The World of
JANE AUSTEN

THE WORLD OF
JANE AUSTEN

NIGEL NICOLSON

PHOTOGRAPHS BY
STEPHEN COLOVER

WEIDENFELD AND NICOLSON
LONDON

First published in 1991 by
George Weidenfeld & Nicolson Limited
Orion House
5 Upper St Martin's Lane
London, WC2H 9EA

Published in paperback 1995

ISBN 0 297 83495 9
Layout by Andrew Shoolbred
House Editor: Suzannah Gough

Frontispiece The Circus, Bath. Designed by the elder John Wood
and executed after his death by his son in 1754–65, it is the
most original and graceful of all their Bath buildings. The circle
of houses, of which no ground-level photograph can show more
than a segment, is unaltered since Jane Austen's day

Printed in Great Britain by
Butler & Tanner Ltd
Frome and London

CONTENTS

The Weald of Kent, seen from the hill on which stands the village of Goudhurst, near Cranbrook. In the middle distance on the left is the isolated church tower of Horsmonden, where several of the early members of the Austen family are buried. The church stands a mile away from its village, next to a cluster of oast-houses where hops are dried. This is the richly cultivated countryside where the Austens lived for centuries before Jane was born and made their modest fortunes, first from iron-smelting and woollen-manufacture (for which the Weald was famous from the fifteenth to the eighteenth centuries) and then from agriculture. Once this was a thickly wooded valley, part of the Wealden forest 'Andredsweald', but in Jane Austen's day its appearance can have been little different from the view shown here.

ACKNOWLEDGEMENTS

My thanks are primarily due to Stephen Colover who took the photographs, and with whom my collaboration and travels have been a constant pleasure; and to Suzannah Gough, our editor, who has matched his pictures to my text with skill and patience.

The authors of the books from which I have derived much information and many ideas are listed in the Bibliography.

The following have been of great help to us. The 'Jane Austen' houses which they own, or with which they are associated, are put in brackets after their names, but in a very few cases they did not wish to be mentioned. Our gratitude to them is nonetheless implicit: Oliver and Mrs Baring (Deane House); Mrs Oliver-Bellasis (Manydown); J. F. Body (Standen); Mrs Deborah Bornoff (Mystole); Miss Jean Bowden (Curator, Jane Austen's House, Chawton); Capt. Michael Boyle (Ashe Park); Viscount Camrose (Hackwood); P. V. Cook (Wyards); Roger Davis (Crabtree Cottage, Surrey); Lord and Lady FitzWalter (Goodnestone); Dr S. Franklin (Basingstoke Museum); John Gillet (Adlestrop); Rev. Martin and Mrs Gillham (Kintbury); Mrs E. Goring (Wrotham); J. David Grey; Mr and Mrs Haydon (Adlestrop); Mrs A. G. and Isolda Hogg (Ibthorpe); Capt. J. D. W. Husband (Chevening); Earl of Iddesleigh (Pynes); Mrs Martin Jackson (Hamstall Ridware); Bryan Keith-Lucas (Wye); Knocker & Foscett, Solicitors (Red House, Sevenoaks); Lord Leigh (Stoneleigh Abbey); Viscount Massareene and Ferrard (Chilham Castle); Adrian Nash (Ashe Park); The National Trust (The Vyne); Landon Platt (Hilsea College); George Plumptre (Rowling); Earl of Portsmouth (Hurstbourne Park); Earl and Countess of Shelburne (Bowood); Bernard Sunley (Godmersham); Mrs E. Tanzer (Grovehurst); Mrs Mathilde Taylor (Goodnestone Dower House); Rev. G. R. Turner (Steventon); Dean of Winchester Cathedral; Alan Wyndham-Green (Godinton).

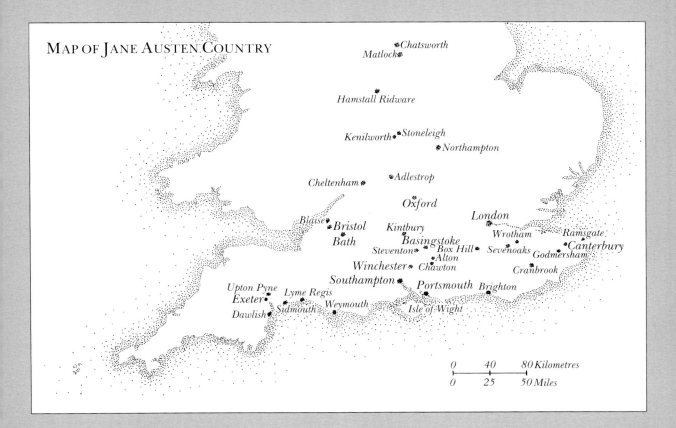

MAP OF JANE AUSTEN COUNTRY

Chatsworth
Matlock

Hamstall Ridware

Kenilworth Stoneleigh
Northampton

Cheltenham   Adlestrop

Oxford

London

Blaise   Kintbury
Bristol   Wrotham   Ramsgate
Bath   Basingstoke   Canterbury
        Steventon   Box Hill   Sevenoaks   Godmersham
Winchester   Alton
        Chawton   Cranbrook
Southampton
Upton Pyne   Portsmouth   Brighton
Exeter   Lyme Regis
Dawlish   Sidmouth   Weymouth   Isle of Wight

0   40   80 Kilometres
0   25   50 Miles

I

JANE AUSTEN'S HOUSES

This book is not a biography of Jane Austen, although it outlines the chief events of her life. Its main purpose is to discuss and illustrate her houses – the houses she lived in and visited, and the houses she invented for her novels – and her love of the English landscape, tamed or wild. I shall not attempt to identify her fictional houses. 'Pemberley' is not Chatsworth, nor 'Rosings' Chevening, though a case has been made out for each. Jane Austen no more drew her houses from life than she did her characters. 'I am too proud of my gentlemen to admit that they were only Mr A or Colonel B', she told a friend. 'Besides, it would be an invasion of social proprieties'. If she made her gentry inhabit recognisable houses, they would be identified with the actual owners. All novelists borrow features, mannerisms and styles of speech and dress from people they know, and amalgamate them to form fictional but believable characters. In the same way, houses which have never existed are invented for the purposes of a story by recollecting details of actual places and fitting them together to create convincing dwellings of several types.

This was Jane Austen's invariable practice. She had no training in architectural history, and it could not be claimed that she was particularly interested in it. One never finds in her letters a close description of a building and seldom an expression of delight at its appearance. She must, for instance, have entered several English cathedrals, but apart from one favourable reference to Winchester's, where she is buried, she never mentions them in her letters or novels, and for the daughter of a parson she is remarkably reticent about the beauty of parish churches: they are simply the work-places of the incumbent where you go to be married in the last chapter. She recognised the main periods of domestic architecture and its development during her lifetime from the Palladian to the Regency, but to her the difference between one house and another was mainly the difference between lifestyles. In an Austen novel a house proclaims its owner's wealth and status less than his taste, for in the late eighteenth-century everything man-made, from a teacup to a portico, was seemly if not beautiful, and the luxury of an apartment was a measure of what its occupant could afford more than of the rightness or originality of his judgement.

In a significant passage of *Pride and Prejudice* Elizabeth Bennet soon wearied of the housekeeper's description of the dining-room at Pemberley, 'a large well-proportioned room, handsomely fitted up' and 'after slightly surveying it, went to a window to enjoy the prospect', as Jane Austen would have done. She loved the English landscape, and almost took for granted the beauty and furnishing of its buildings.

However, she noticed more than she perhaps realised. She made use of houses, streets and gardens as stage-sets for her people to move into and around. She is never guilty of an anachronism or an error of scale (slapping a bow-window onto an Elizabethan hall or a Van Dyck into a vicarage), and knows from experience how a small room can be cleared for a dance or a library for amateur theatricals. She makes use of the subtle difference between a drawing-room and a saloon as an indication of class, and knows how to place the servants, in what rooms and at what time of day. She correctly gauges how much noise would penetrate from a dinner party to an upper bedroom, and how much of the carriage-drive would be visible from the bedroom's windows. Domestic details of this sort are essential ingredients of her plots. Rooms separate people from each other, or bring them convivially together: the stairs and corridors create accidental meetings, the shrubbery an opportunity for an intimate conversation. There is much movement in a Jane Austen novel, and it all occurs within a carefully contrived scenario. It is nonetheless selective. The heroine rarely leaves the drawing-room for the kitchen. We never see her in bed. The squalors and inconveniences of an eighteenth-century house are ignored. A horse goes lame once, in *Emma*, and a carriage overturns in *Sanditon*, but the life of a rectory or great house runs almost too smoothly to be true. Servants never fall ill or give notice; meals always arrive on time; the crockery remains for generations intact; people are sometimes said to have died, but never in the course of the story; and with the important exceptions of Louisa Musgrove's fall in *Persuasion* and Jane Bennet's cold, there is no pain and almost no sickness. It is a sanatised world in which the only unpleasantness lies in human nature.

The novels describe the dwellings of a wide social group, from a widow's two-roomed flat in an unsalubrious quarter of Bath to a country house fit for an earl, but she does not stray outside these parameters, not because she was ignorant of the interior of a working man's cottage nor, for that matter, of the Prince Regent's library in Carlton House, but because she was uncertain how people of that kind behaved and

Previous page Ibthorpe House, near Hurstbourne Tarrant, Hampshire, the home of Martha and Mary Lloyd, with whom Jane Austen often stayed. It is a perfect early Georgian house, which she might have taken as a model for many of the smaller houses described in her novels.

talked in private, just as she avoids the conversation of men apart from women. She would write only of what she knew from experience. In fact, her own world was more enlarged than that which she invents. Anyone who has visited some of the many places she knew, or seen them illustrated in *Jane Austen's England* by Maggie Lane or *In the Steps of Jane Austen* by Anne-Marie Edwards (to both of which books I am much indebted) will know that while a small Georgian house like Ibthorpe or a roomy rectory like Adlestrop was where she felt most comfortable, she could live, and write, happily in crowded, shapeless, noisy little houses like Steventon or Chawton, and feel quite unintimidated, even as a young girl, in so grand a house as Hackwood. Being innocent of snobbishness or pretence herself, she could detect both at all social levels, and enjoyed the wide variety of the company she kept as much as the variety of the places they inhabited.

Considering that England was engaged in a desperate war for all but the last two years of her adult life, she was able to travel quite widely, even to the south coast when it was threatened with invasion. She never went abroad, never to Scotland or Ireland nor (as far as we know) to Wales, but in England she knew well every southern county from Kent

Cottages near Deane House, barely a mile from Steventon where Jane Austen was born and spent the first twenty-five years of her life. Although they have been spruced up since her day, this is the type of eighteenth-century cottage in her father's parish which she visited on charitable errands, but in her novels the rural poor play only walk-on parts.

13

to Devon, ventured at least as far north as Staffordshire, and lived for periods of several months or years in London, Bath and Southampton. She never saw a major lake or moor, an industrial town, a mountain or a mine, and the English countryside must have appeared to her unvaryingly gentle and attractive. The difficulties of travel two centuries ago were no deterrent to the Austens. They would cheerfully embark on a three-day journey without knowing whether the public coach could take them or the inns have rooms available for night-stops. They thought eight miles an hour and sixty miles a day on a turnpike good going (in correcting the novel of her niece Anna, Jane wrote, 'They must be *two* days going from Dawlish to Bath: they are nearly 100 miles apart'). They expected lanes to be impassable in winter except on horseback or on foot with clogs. Night travel was very hazardous except under an unclouded full moon. On the other hand, the turnpikes were by now relatively smooth: Jane could read to her brother Henry the manuscript of *Mansfield Park* on a coach-journey from Alton to London, and a Wedgwood dinner-service was sent in the reverse direction without breakage.

The leisurely pace of travel allowed Jane Austen to look around her at the countryside and market squares where the coachman changed horses and his passengers ate. She added to her mental store of architectural styles by observing the town and country houses which they passed. She was not by nature an addicted tourist, but one can deduce from the habits of her fictional characters that she would sometimes

Opposite The Vyne, Hampshire. The main entrance is flanked by stone eagles presented to John Chute by Horace Walpole. This was one of the houses near Basingstoke where Jane Austen went for dances and gathered her information about how people lived in grander houses.

Above The London to Dartford stage-coach, painted by J. Cordrey in 1813. Jane and Cassandra Austen would often have been among its passengers on their way to their brother's house in mid-Kent, for although 'travelling stage' was not considered ladylike, they were indifferent to snobbishness of this kind and tolerant of the discomforts of the journey.

turn off the road to visit castles and abbeys and even private houses where the 'polite stranger' would be admitted at stated hours, just as Elizabeth and the Gardiners call unannounced and unexpected at Pemberley. Chatsworth, for example, was open two days a week, Blenheim from two o'clock till four o'clock, and at Kedleston Lord Scarsdale went so far as to build an inn 'for the accommodation of such strangers as curiosity may lead to view his residence.'

Primarily Jane Austen was a walker. Being country-bred and country-loving, she gladly and easily escaped the town when forced to live in one, and towns were then small. You could walk from end to end of London in an afternoon, and Chelsea, where she often stayed with her brother, was surrounded by open fields. Ten minutes' walk would take her clear of her two other towns, Bath and Southampton. Healthy, active and unorthodox, she laughed away the convention that young women should not appear in drawing-rooms with skirt-hems dripping mud, which Miss Bingley considered to show 'an abominable sort of conceited independence, a most country-town indifference to decorum'. She would walk from village to village along the crests, noting as she did not only the pleasantness of dipping wooded hills, but little churches cupped in the dells, and the cottages and larger houses which composed her ideal communities in life as in her fiction, like Uppercross in *Persuasion*:

> a moderate-sized village, which a few years back had been completely in the old English style, containing only two houses superior in appearance to those of the yeoman and labourers – the mansion of the squire, with its high walls, great gates and old trees, substantial and unmodernised, and the compact tight parsonage, enclosed in its own neat garden, with a vine and a pear-tree trained round its casements; but upon the marriage of the young squire, it had received the improvement of a farmhouse elevated into a cottage for his residence, and Uppercross Cottage, with its veranda, French windows and other prettinesses was quite as likely to catch the traveller's eye as the more consistent and considerable aspect and premises of the Great House.

There are few better examples of how the Englishness of England and her observation of changing styles, seeped into her novels. Here is another, her description of the setting of Donwell Abbey in *Emma*:

> The considerable slope, at nearly the foot of which the Abbey stood, gradually acquired a steeper form beyond its grounds; and at half a

The flowing gowns and light slippers of the period were no deterrent to the walks which Jane Austen enjoyed, wherever she found herself within reach of the open countryside.

MORNING DRESS.

mile distant was a bank of considerable abruptness and grandeur, well clothed with wood; and at the bottom of this bank, favourably placed and sheltered, rose the Abbey-Mill Farm, with meadows in front, and the river making a close and handsome curve around it.

It was a sweet view – sweet to the eye and the mind. English verdure, English culture, English comfort, seen under a sun bright without being offensive.

She might have been describing the view from the garden of Gilbert White's Selborne, only four miles from Chawton. Like him, she was an intense patriot. Knowing no other country, she could imagine none more delightful.

Jane was only forty-one when she died and was totally unknown to the general public, for she published only four novels in her lifetime and those anonymously. In December 1817, only five months after her death, her brother Henry published *Northanger Abbey* and *Persuasion* under her true name and added a biographical note about her. Although from the time of Bentley's edition in 1833 the novels were uninterruptedly in print, 'it was a private rather than a public reputation' as Brian Southam has said, 'sustained within families and literary circles', and only with the publication in 1869 of the *Memoir* by her nephew James Edward Austen-Leigh did interest in her as a person begin to stir, and it has given rise to such extended research that not a year passes without several books being added to her already immense bibliography.

Though she and her sister Cassandra never married, five of her brothers did, four of them twice, and at her death Jane had twenty-three nephews and nieces. Family affection for her extended to the third and fourth generations, and when first-hand memories were extinguished, the scholars took over. Her letters were disinterred, expurgated and published, archives of families known to her were ransacked for any mention of her, and as early as 1902 a book was written about the houses she had lived in or visited, *Jane Austen: Her Homes and Her Friends*. So famous had she become that the biography of two distinguished admirals, Francis and Charles Austen, had to be published under the title *Jane Austen's Sailor Brothers* to command the attention of reviewers.

The evidence, however, can never be complete, and in attempting to assess her knowledge of English towns and country houses, one is obliged often to speculate. Some episodes in her life, indeed whole years, are but lightly documented, like a crossword puzzle tentatively

Left Mrs George Austen, Jane's excellent mother, a humorous woman, practical, energetic, with a lively imagination that she transmitted to her younger daughter.

Below Rev. George Austen, a miniature painted in 1801. A handsome, placid man, he was a good scholar and a loving father, to whom Jane owed her serenity and the refinement of her intellect.

pencilled in. Her letters to Cassandra were partly destroyed by her, and other members of the Austen family were even more protective or careless – it is difficult to determine which – for we know of no letters to either of her parents, none to her brothers James, Edward or Henry, and only one to Charles, though hundreds must have been written. From the end of May 1801 until 1805, the Bath period, only a single letter survives. Much has been made of the triviality of her letters, their concern with the minutiae of clothes, food, gossip and family arrangements, and of their artless language (compared, say, to Charlotte Brontë's, which are as mellifluous as her published prose), for she flits from subject to subject, prattling as she goes, writing helter-skelter to inform and amuse, and as in most letters intended for only one pair of eyes, there are digs and nudges at other people, some affectionate ('Dear Mrs Digweed! I cannot bear that she should not be foolishly happy after a ball'), some less so, ('She was highly rouged, and looked rather quietly and contently silly') and some downright coarse, ('Mrs Hall was brought to bed yesterday of a dead child, owing to a fright. I suppose she happened unawares to look at her husband', a sentence that has shocked generations of Janeites).

Her dominant mood was playful raillery. She was lively, robust, graceful, critical, witty and benevolent. 'No one could be often in her company', wrote her brother Henry, 'without feeling a strong desire of obtaining her friendship', and this rings true. She lived in a world where good manners and intellectual excellence were held to be admirable, but these virtues must be allied to vigour, daring, tenderness and a capacity for love and disdain, the qualities in fact which she gives to her favourite heroines. Although she wrote her novels primarily to amuse herself and us, she had another purpose. It was didactic. She wished us to consider goodness and badness, the virtue that a fine man can personify without loss of manliness, and the mettle of a young woman without sacrifice of her femininity, and in both of them the flaws which we all inadvertently reveal. She examined the hierarchy of the English eighteenth century, its rigid class system, social cruelties and hypocrisies, but also its merits, its approximation to a perfect society, its culture and its taste, for although she rarely uses the word, it is implicit in one of her titles, *Sense and Sensibility*, sense meaning decorum, wisdom and a certain harmony in our manner, and sensibility standing for zest and spirit. Excellence, she considered, is innate: it cannot be acquired or bought, and however much innocence is abused, it will always triumph in the end. Jane Austen was not much abused: life treated her well apart from an early death. She was greatly loved, endured few disappointments, and when she died there was nothing with which she needed to reproach herself.

Cassandra Austen, Jane's devoted elder sister. Their mother said of them, 'If Cassandra were going to have her head cut off, Jane would insist on sharing her fate'.

This book attempts more than a description of the places she knew and their transformation into the places she imagined. I have visited all the houses which meant a great deal to her and some with which she had but a passing acquaintance, and where they no longer exist, have substituted old prints and drawings. But if limited to that, the book would turn out to be little more than the catalogue of a Regency estate agent. My purpose has also been to consider her novels as a product of her experience. So profound a knowledge of human nature as she showed in her writing from an astonishingly early age could only have come from mixing with many people. In the same way, her unfaltering sense of place is the distillation of close observation and a photographic mind. It is her gift for combining the two, putting people into places, that forms the theme of this book.

II

EARLY YEARS IN HAMPSHIRE

Jane Austen was born on 16 December 1775 in her father's parsonage at Steventon, a small village five miles from Basingstoke, and it remained her home for the next twenty-five years until her father decided suddenly to retire to Bath. It was at Steventon and on holidays in different parts of Hampshire and Kent that she drafted her first three novels, *Sense and Sensibility*, *Pride and Prejudice* and *Northanger Abbey*, all between the ages of nineteen and twenty-three.

George Austen's parsonage or rectory was pulled down not many years after her death because it had become too decrepit in the eyes of his successor, his own son Henry, and today its site is the corner of a field marked only by the iron pump which stood in the Austen's courtyard, now guarded against the cows by ugly railings. Behind it, higher up the slope, are traces in the turf of terracing where they contrived a short walk across the top of their modest garden. Beyond the hedge were the few fields that George Austen farmed. The situation was agreeable but by no means idyllic. This part of Hampshire is decently but dully undulating, the fields too large for their hedges to form interesting patterns, the hills unspectacular, while Steventon itself was more a line of cottages than a village, the church and manor house standing half a mile from where its centre ought to be.

The parsonage was quite large and had a certain style. We have two drawings of it, front and back, done by Anna Austen, James's daughter, in about 1814, and they indicate something of its huggermugger amplitude and modest pretensions to gentility. There is a short approach drive to a latticed front door, and the windows, one or two to a room, show how their large family was packed in. There were two parlours and a kitchen, a private study for the Vicar and ten bedrooms above, three of them in the attics. Jane and Cassandra shared a bedroom, as they continued to do in other houses all their lives, but they had a 'dressing-room' where Jane kept her pianoforte and, one supposes, wrote.

Given the lack of privacy, of lavatories, running water, adequate lighting and any method of preserving perishable food except by salting

Back front of Steventon Rectory. 1814

Previous page The site of Steventon Rectory from the field numbered 8 in the plan on page 25. The house stood to the right of the tallest tree, and its only relic is the courtyard pump now enclosed by railings. The road on the left led to Steventon church where Jane's father officiated.

The front and back of Steventon Rectory, drawings by Anna Austen. It was here that Jane Austen was born in 1775 and lived half her life. The house was roomy but internally a bit ramshackle, and it was demolished by her brother in 1828.

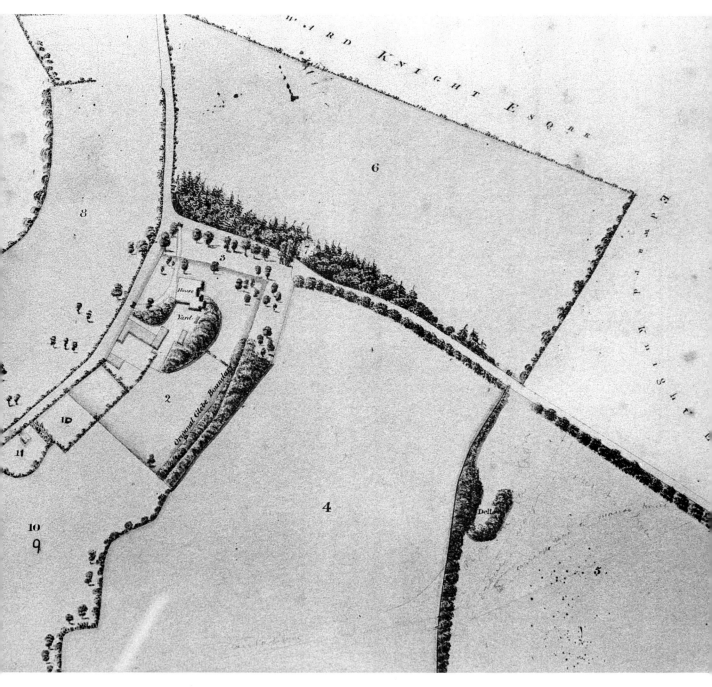

A plan of the Glebe land at Steventon in 1821. The
Rectory lies nearest the road-junction, and the
numbered fields are those owned and farmed by George
Austen to supplement his vicar's stipend. The Glebe
land is bordered by property belonging to his son
Edward who took the name of Knight from his adopting
parents.

or smoking, and a household which at times amounted to fifteen people counting servants and the students whom the Vicar enrolled to supplement his stipend, only remarkable good temper and forebearance can have made life tolerable. None of Jane's fictional families except the Prices of Portsmouth lived so much on top of one another. But it was more than tolerable: it was exuberant and intensely affectionate. All the Austens except one mentally backward son were alert people, as playful as they were industrious, ambitious in the least obnoxious way, humorous, companionable and above all good-natured. Their father, Rev. George Austen, was handsome in feature, energetic, intelligent and profoundly attached to his children. His tolerance is shown in his attitude to Jane's early writing. Far from putting it aside as a childhood fantasy, he encouraged her, laughed with her over her mounting roll-call of real or imaginary characters, and when she produced a full-length novel, *First Impressions*, (later to become *Pride and Prejudice*), which contained literature's most brilliant lampoon of a foolish clergyman, he offered it to Cadell's for publication 'at the author's expense' and shared her disappointment when it was refused. Jane's mother, born Cassandra Leigh, was shrewd, high-minded, determined and capable, with a strong sense of humour and an attachment to her children which equalled her husband's and their love for each other. It was a family exceptional for its mutual support and lifelong cohesiveness.

Their occupations at Steventon were those of any middle-class family: household chores, drawing, reading aloud, music-making, sewing, card-playing, amateur theatricals, church-going, walking, shooting and riding for the boys, and for all of them visiting and being visited. Their treats were not concerts, theatres or seaside holidays (at least, not yet) but dances. It was dancing, and friendships nurtured on the dance-floor, that took Jane Austen away from the ramshackle rectory into a wider society, and who can doubt that her novels originated in the family's jovial postmortems on the parties they attended and the odd people they met, for they shared an ironic view of the world, delighted in the ridiculous, and balanced propriety with irreverence in a wholly healthy proportion. At the same time, they were left in no doubt that the life they enjoyed was privileged. Jane well understood the hardships of the rural poor, which in her lifetime, as William Cobbett constantly reminded the gentry, were extreme. She was excellently placed to observe English society upward and downward, humble enough to meet the villagers on terms not intimidating to them, refined and bright enough to associate with the minor and not so minor aristocracy without awe or awkwardness. Like Elizabeth Bennet, 'there was a mixture of sweetness and archness in her manner which made it difficult for her to affront anybody'.

Her appearance, as well as her natural high spirits and curiosity about people, gave her confidence. She was exceptionally attractive. It is unfortunate that the only two portraits we have of her are sketches by her sister which do her less than justice. The more unfamiliar of the two shows her from behind, her features and body so concealed by her voluminous clothes and bonnet that it might be a sketch of any woman of any age from sixteen to sixty, when in fact she was about twenty-seven when it was made. The second, drawn some nine years later, is even more misleading, for where is the intelligence, the humour, the imagination, the *kindness* in those dim eyes and pinched lips beneath the mob cap? It contradicts every account we have of her, like Mrs

Above The only known representation of Jane's features, a watercolour by Cassandra done in about 1810 when Jane was thirty-five.

Right This watercolour of Jane Austen was drawn by her sister Cassandra in about 1802. It is authenticated by a letter from Anna Austen (Lefroy) in 1862 which refers to 'a sketch which Aunt Cassandra made of her on one of their expeditions – sitting down out of doors on a hot day, with her bonnet strings untied'.

Beckford's, 'I remember her as a tall thin *spare* person, with very high cheekbones, great colour, sparkling eyes not large but joyous and intelligent', or the Rev. Fowle's in conversation with a friend, the more convincing because it is hesitant: 'Pretty – certainly pretty – bright and a good deal of colour in her face – like a doll – no, that would not give at all the idea, for she had so much expression – she was like a child – quite a child, very lively and full of humour – most amiable, most beloved'; and finally her niece Caroline's first-hand testimony, 'She was not an absolute beauty, but before she left Steventon she was established as a very pretty girl.' She enjoyed her own delectability, dressed with design, and she could attract and flirt. The importance she attaches in her novels to the handsomeness of her heroes and the beauty of her heroines (not only from the neck up) is an indication of the pleasure she took in a good appearance. She was not without vanity. 'A pleasing young woman' was how a friend described her to Cassandra, who repeated the compliment. 'Well', commented Jane, who was then thirty-five, 'that must do: one cannot pretend to anything better now, thankful to having it continued a few years longer.'

Much as she enjoyed party-going, it was no part of her doctrine that the grander the party the better. She knew that the dullest occasions were often found in the smartest houses, as at Lady Middleton's in *Sense and Sensibility*, where the insipidity of the conversation 'produced not one novelty of thought or expression'. What she most enjoyed was a small, lively dinner-party followed by an impromptu dance, and a visit to or from the most attractive guest next morning. She based the most significant scenes in her novels on such occasions, advancing the plot mostly by conversation. Her ear was astonishingly receptive and retentive, for how otherwise, aged twenty or little more, could she have invented conversations so subtle in thought and so beautifully balanced in language unless she had experienced and contributed to them? Indeed was she not improving on them, since few of her friends could have been capable of so spontaneous, melodious and epigrammatic a style as Emma or Henry Crawford, who expressed themselves so well that in real life we would need thirty seconds pause between each sentence while we shaped the next?

The neighbourhood of Basingstoke was well suited to the upbringing of a novelist intent on reproducing, half-satirically, the society of the upper-middle class and clergy. The mix of rank, their varied dwellings, the scattering of villages round a small market town afforded all she needed for plotting her simple stories and expressing her moral attitudes. One is aware of a wickeder world outside, in large towns and seaports, and she does not wholly suppress the distant boom of naval gunfire, specially in *Persuasion*, but her books are mainly concerned with the normal and apparently immutable style of English country living where nothing much happens except the slow shift in the relationship of one young person to another.

There was only a difference of eight years between the five youngest Austen children. They grew up together, shared the same friendships, visited the same houses – Steventon Manor, Ashe Park, Ashe House, Deane, Manydown, Oakley Hall, and then the grander quintet – Hackwood, Hurstbourne Park, The Vyne, Kempshott Park and Laverstoke. There were several others. When Mrs Bennet boasts, 'We dine out with four and twenty families', the same could have been said of the Austens. It was probably a wider selection of houses than most vicarage children would enjoy today when communication between them is easier and class distinctions less rigid. Just because the badness of the roads confined people to their immediate neighbourhood in winter, and to the range of a pony-cart in summer, and because they lacked any other form of social entertainment (no tennis, no swimming pools), they tended to make the most of their close group, even the higher aristocracy among them, though the peers did not expect to be invited back to the parsonages.

We hear, for example, of the Lords Portsmouth, Dorchester and Bolton attending a ball at the Angel Inn at Basingstoke where sixty

The Angel Inn, Basingstoke, in 1862, from the Inn's letterhead of that date. It was in the Assembly Room above the stables that the neighbours gathered in the winter for monthly dances. It could hold up to thirty couples.

people were packed into the 'Assembly Rooms', a large hall above the stables and coach-house, later to become a hayloft with the old chandelier still swinging above the hay, but demolished when Basingstoke became so pleased with its present that it forgot its past. Dances were held there once a month during the Season, and there can be little doubt that in describing the dance at Meryton when Darcy snubbed Elizabeth, Jane Austen was drawing directly upon them. The scene in the novel resembles too exactly the scene as she described it for Cassandra at Christmas 1798: 'Mr Calland, who appeared as usual with his hat in his hand, stood every now and then behind Catherine and me to be talked to and abused for not dancing. We teased him, however, into it at last.' About another ball she wrote, 'There were more dancers than the room could hold. I do not think I was very much in request. People were apt rather not to ask me if they could help it.' One catches the mocking and self-mocking style which may account for her shortage of partners. But there was another motive in her eagerness. All dances are courtships of a kind. 'To be fond of dancing', pontificates Sir William Lucas in *Pride and Prejudice*, 'was a certain step towards falling in love.'

We know of one serious flirtation, and one proposal, during the Steventon days, each linked with a house that came to mean much to her.

The flirtation was with Tom Lefroy, a handsome young Irishman, nephew of the Rev. George Lefroy, Rector of Ashe, a village within walking distance of Steventon. Jane spoke and wrote of him in a jocular, off-hand manner which revealed her more serious attraction.

> I am almost afraid to tell you, [she told her sister in the very first of her letters to survive, dated January 1796,] how my Irish friend and I behaved. Imagine to yourself everything most profligate and shocking in the way of dancing and sitting down together. I *can* expose myself, however, only *once more*, because he leaves the country soon after next Friday, on which day we *are* to have a dance at Ashe after all. He is a very gentleman-like, good-looking, pleasant young man, I assure you.

A week or two later he left Hampshire and she never saw him again, but in old age, when he was Chief Justice of Ireland, he looked back fondly on his youthful escapade, and admitted that he had loved her, 'but it was only a boy's love'.

The point, however, is not this brief affair, but the house and its mistress, Anne Lefroy. Ashe Rectory (now renamed Ashe House) still

A ball dress of the period.

The drawing-room at
Goodnestone Park, Kent,
where Jane Austen danced
while on visits to her
brother Edward, who
married the daughter of
the house, Elizabeth
Bridges. It was in country-
houses like this that about
five couples could stage *ex
tempore* dances after dinner.

Opposite page The drawing-room at Ashe House, seen from the dining-room. The doors are those which were folded back to make room for dancing. On other evenings, Jane tells us, the rooms were used for card-playing and 'casino'.

Below Ashe House, near Steventon, was formerly the Rectory of the neighbouring parish, and it was here that Jane met the Rector's wife, Anne Lefroy, who was to have such a great influence on her intellectual development.

Left Mrs Lefroy, whom Jane described as 'a perfect model of gracefulness and goodness'.

Manydown House, where Jane was briefly engaged to marry its heir, Harris Bigg-Wither, but after a night's reflection she retracted her promise because she could not love him. The print (*above*) was made in her day, and the photograph taken shortly before the demolition of the house in 1965.

stands. It is one of the prettiest Georgian houses that Jane knew, and she knew it intimately. Its smiling countenance seen from the lane gives an immediate impression of welcome which is confirmed inside, where sitting-rooms open hospitably each side of the hall, one of them expanding by folding doors into the dining-room, the same doors which were swung back in Jane's day to make the two rooms into one for dancing. For at least three nights in 1815 she slept there in the comfort which guests still enjoy. The furniture is different, the fabrics are of newer design, and there is every modern electronic aid, but no house that I visited in the course of this enquiry recalled more pleasantly the grace of the middle-sized country house which she so often extolled. Mrs Lefroy was more to her than an older friend. Jane could talk to her as she could talk to no other person even in her family, finding in her the perfect recipient of her confidences and literary ambitions, and when Mrs Lefroy died in 1804, killed in a riding accident, Jane felt it as a personal calamity. The love she had for two people in this house, the Irish boy and his charming aunt, make a visit to it a moving experience.

The 'engagement' was at Manydown House, where the Austen girls often stayed for the Basingstoke dances, and her 'fiancé' of twelve hours was the son of the house, Harris Bigg-Wither, whose three sisters, Alethea, Catherine and Elizabeth were among the Austens' intimates. It was at Manydown in January 1796 that Jane had flirted with Tom Lefroy, and six years later, when she was twenty-seven, she stayed there on holiday from Bath. Harris proposed to her and was accepted. Cassandra, who was also in the house at the time, strangely approved of the engagement, not because Jane loved him (he was rather unloveable, six years younger than her, overgrown, awkward, with a stammer) but because by marrying him she would become mistress of a considerable estate. After a night agonising over what she had promised so hastily, she broke off the engagement and left the house. She would not have been happy there. Harris was a heavy sort of youth and Manydown a heavy sort of house, with an Elizabethan wing forming one side of an inner courtyard. Inside a grand staircase swept up to a large drawing-room where the dances were held. It was undistinguished, but when in 1965 it was proposed to pull it down after the family had failed to attract any offers for it, even as a gift, there was an outcry from Janeites that it was unthinkable to destroy a place of which Jane Austen might have become chatelaine. But as none of them came forward with an offer to pay for its restoration, destroyed it was, and old photographs must now do duty for the reality.

Much more attractive, and still beautifully preserved, is Deane House. It had particular associations for the Austens, for the Rev

George was for a time vicar of this parish as well as of Steventon, and his elder children were born in its Rectory within sight of the manor house. It had belonged to the Harwood family for five or six generations, and its present owner, John Harwood, lived there in a style far above his income, a fact which his family discovered, to their dismay, only after his death in 1813. In his lifetime it was a centre of local society. A long low brick house, probably late seventeenth-century in origin and altered and improved in the three succeeding centuries, it is a lovely sight in summer, standing at the head of a great lawn with a pale church to one side of it. Jane Austen began her account of one of the many dances she attended there with the statement, 'There were but fifty people in the room', as if fifty was an unexpectedly small number for a dance at Deane, and she exercised her wit on most of them – 'broad face, diamond bandeau, white shoes, pink husband and fat neck; I was as civil to them as their bad breath would allow me' – but she leaves unexplained, as Cassandra did not need telling, how so numerous a company fitted into the intimate rooms of this charming house. The long drawing-room is a nineteenth-century addition. Was there an equivalent saloon on its site in 1800? Constance Hill, visiting the house in 1902, is no help. She suggests the panelled dining-room. It could barely contain ten couples.

To the Austens the third most important house in the constellation round Steventon was Ashe Park. It belonged to William Portal, who let it from about 1790 to James Holder, a bachelor with a West Indian fortune, like Sir Thomas Bertram of Mansfield Park. Jane, who did not often express pleasure in comfort, wrote of it in 1800, 'To sit in idleness over a good fire in a well-proportioned room is a luxurious sensation. Sometimes we talked and sometimes we were quite silent. I said two or three amusing things, and Mr Holder made a few infamous puns.' But she did not wholly trust her host. A year later she arrived at the house ahead of the main party, 'and was shut up in the drawing-room with Mr Holder alone for ten minutes. I had some thought of insisting on the housekeeper or Mary Corbett [a maid] being sent for, and nothing could prevail on me to move two steps from the door, on the lock of which I kept one hand constantly fixed'. There are other references to card-playing and dinner parties of fourteen at Ashe, but not dancing. Mr Holder did not dance.

Where was the well-proportioned room, and where the drawing-room with its convenient door-knob? Two-thirds of the present house is a Victorian reconstruction, and none of the rooms where Jane sat survives entire. This is clear from the brickwork and the style. The contemporary print reproduced on page 40 shows a different, smaller

Deane House, the property of John Harwood, is the archetypal Jane Austen house, a generous, welcoming, red-brick house near the parish church. Here were held many of the parties on which Jane based, for example, the Westons' dance in *Emma*.

house of which only the service wing stands, incorporating the present dining-room, identifiable in the print as the room with the bow-window before it was enlarged by throwing into it a neighbouring sitting-room. This was the room, perhaps, which she so much admired, but the drawing-room was replaced by a more magnificent one in about 1850.

The Elizabethan manor house, close by Steventon church, was rented by the Digweed family from the Knights of Godmersham, Kent, and used by them as a farmhouse. It was in a condition so decrepit that it seems to have made little impression on Jane except as a curiosity. Its stone porch, heavy mullioned windows and great chimney stack wreathed in ivy (I quote from Constance Hill's description in 1902) might have suggested to her the perfect setting for a Gothic story had she possessed that cast of mind, but she didn't. When she came to praise an Elizabethan manor like Sotherton Court in *Mansfield Park*, it was not in the least like Steventon's, but 'a noble old place ... a large regular brick building but respectable looking and has many good

Ashe Park as it was in Jane Austen's day. The room which she so much admired is probably that with the bow windows, and it is incorporated in the present dining-room.

rooms'. She would not have regretted the fate of the Digweed house. It was extensively rebuilt in the mid-nineteenth century, burnt in 1932, rebuilt again and demolished in the 1970s.

There was finally, in this category, Oakley Hall (now Hilsea College), a house built in the year of the French Revolution. It is intact today but disfigured by a 1860 *porte cochère* and a look of weariness which comes from occupation by a generation of school children. The interior is superior to the exterior. The owners were Jane's friend Wither Bramston and his eccentric sister Augusta who is best remembered for her outspoken comments on Jane's books, 'She owned that she thought S & S and P & P downright nonsense but expected to like M P better, and having finished the first volume, flattered herself that she had got through the worst'.

Outside this group of half-a-dozen houses where Jane in her childhood and youth was so much at her ease that she could knock on their doors uninvited, was a circle of houses of the first rank, works of

The garden front of Oakley Hall (now Hilsea College) which was rebuilt in 1789 for the Bramston family. It is another of the surviving houses round Basingstoke where the Austens were frequently guests.

Hackwood, the grandest house which Jane Austen knew in her youth. In the late eighteenth century Lord Bolton, who owned it, would not think it unusual to invite to his splendid parties the daughters of an insignificant parson, and Jane took such entertainments in her stride and as material for her novels. The equestrian lead statue is of George I, a present from the King to the 3rd Duke of Bolton.

Following page Hurstbourne Park, the seat of the Earl of Portsmouth who had been George Austen's pupil at Steventon and maintained his friendship with the family by inviting them to his annual balls. In 1800 Jane wrote to her sister, 'I believe I drank too much wine last night at Hurstbourne. I know not how else to account for the shaking of my hand.' The house, by James Wyatt, was burned down in 1870.

architecture instead of the copybook artifices of local builders, and the Austens were often invited to them as guests at annual dances, a wedding or a garden party. Jane was unimpressed by them. She seems not to have considered them particularly beautiful. The fine furniture and pictures seemed to her little removed from ostentation, and grandness of housing was apt to induce a grandness of manner which she found absurd. So much at least one deduces from the novels, and from the absence of any sense of awe or admiration in her description of such scenes to her equally indifferent sister. Their visits are important in her life and art because they made her familiar with the patrician interiors of great houses and a new level of society. She learnt from them how the aristocracy live, and therefore, to some extent, how they thought.

Take, for example, the grandest of them all, Hackwood, just south of Basingstoke. In origin a late-seventeenth-century house it was remodelled for the first and second Lord Boltons in the early 1800s by Lewis Wyatt. As Jane Austen mentions the 'Hackwood balls' in 1799 as events that have occurred or are occurring, it is probable that she saw the unaltered house before its centre was doubled to the thickness of two great rooms, and that she danced in the ballroom at the east end of the south front, now an indoor swimming pool. She knew Lord Bolton from his visits to Manydown and the Basingstoke Assembly Room, but the acquaintance was slight and perhaps unrewarding, for he was said to be interested more in pigs than people and visited their fine styes every morning. Hackwood is more famous for its garden than the house. Magnificent though it is, it is in a sense anachronistic in its late Palladianism which by 1800 had almost exhausted its possibilities, and the façades need, and are given, fondling by trees and shadows to relieve their austerity. The main rooms are large and numerous, as if the architect had to devise uses for them to extend the ground floor as a foundation for the countless bedrooms above, but their grandeur is justified by their elegance, particularly the saloon's, a large room of excellent proportions, with ivory-coloured walls and gold-leafed cornices. If Jane Austen saw it as we see it, she could have stored it in her memory as a sketch for the drawing-room at Rosings, which was large enough for the inhabitants to engage in separate activities in different parts of it and a shy guest to hide.

Another house of comparable size was Hurstbourne Park, the seat of the Earl of Portsmouth, five miles east of Andover on the Basingstoke road. The connection here was closer: the Earl, as Lord Lymington, had been George Austen's pupil in 1773 and never failed to invite the family to his annual ball at Hurstbourne. Later he grew so 'unpleasantly eccentric', according to William Austen-Leigh, that he was declared a

Laverstoke House, built in
1796–8 for Henry Portal by
Joseph Bonomi, the only
architect whom Jane
mentions by name (not
agreeably) in her novels. She
probably saw the house in
course of construction and
visited it again in 1815.

lunatic in 1823. His house was impeccably sane, a central pile with two wings joined to it by curving arms, each wing substantial enough to stand as a fine country house by itself. The park was landscaped to include a lake and groves of oak and beech on the nearer hills. The mansion no longer exists. It was burned down in 1870, and its replacement was itself demolished in 1965.

Near Hurstbourne was Laverstoke House, an important landmark in Jane's architectural education for it was under construction at the very period when she knew it, and by the only architect whom she mentions by name in her novels, Joseph Bonomi. Her family connection with it was through the marriage in 1792 of her elder brother James to Anne Mathew, the daughter of the fiery General Edward Mathew, ex-Governor of Grenada, who rented the old manor of Laverstoke from Joseph Portal. James's daughter Anna was given a lavish christening party there. Portal's son Harry pulled down the old house and on a new site built the much grander Laverstoke House in 1796–8. Its most striking external features are a giant portico of slender unfluted Ionic columns and an Italianate arched bell-tower behind. The interior is superb, with a double staircase under Bonomi's oval skylight, a long drawing-room and a library. One would wish to have had Jane's opinion of it, but it is unlikely to have been favourable, as when she came to mention Bonomi in *Sense and Sensibility*, she makes Robert

Freefolk Priors, the home of generations of the Portal family, which was rented from them by General Edward Mathew whose daughter Anne married James Austen in 1792. The house, which lay in the park at Laverstoke, was demolished in 1851. From *Select Illustrations of Hampshire*, 1833.

Ferrars throw into the fire three of Bonomi's plans for a new house for Lord Courtland and advise him to build a cottage instead. She was not sympathetic to change. She was also a xenophobic. Bonomi was born Italian.

The Vyne is the finest of the north Hampshire houses she knew, and the least altered. The present disposition of the main rooms, though not in every case their uses, and much of the furnishing and pictures, are what she would have recognised, even if in the hands of the National Trust it is cleaner and less cluttered than in the Chutes's. The house dates largely from the reign of Henry VIII. Later alterations were made boldly but sympathetically, like John Webb's portico, the first to be attached to any English country house, and the theatrical, ice-cool staircase which John Chute, the friend of Horace Walpole, designed within the confines of the hall. James Austen became the vicar of the neighbouring parish, and it was through his friendship with the family that Jane too was their occasional visitor. We know from Mrs Chute's diary, for example, that she dined there in April 1799, and there are vague indications that she danced there too. But where? Hitherto the assumption had been that the ball must have been staged in the famous Tudor long gallery, but we know from the journal of Caroline Wiggett, whom the Chutes adopted as a real-life Fanny Price, that the gallery was a lumber-room and her playroom, and one of the drawing-rooms must have been cleared for the occasion. It was a rare event. The quietness and uneventfulness of this well-off family, even though William Chute was Master of The Vyne Hunt and MP for Hampshire, correct the impression of the novels that country houses pulsated with activity and drama. The Chutes gave only two or three dinner parties a year, and in winter, wrote Caroline in recollection, 'the roads had ruts deep enough to bury me in', so that excursions were only possible in summer. In winter, while the men hunted, the women sang and sewed, and pasted up pictures on the print room walls.

It is in keeping with Jane Austen's habits and character to bring her back to the sort of society and the type of house she preferred in her early Hampshire years. Ibthorpe House, near Hurstbourne Tarrant, south of Newbury, is the archetypal Austen house. Lying at the further edge of an exceptionally pretty village, in countryside which is grander in relief and fluffier with trailing woods than the country round Steventon, Ibthorpe has in common with Ashe House a glowing, open, friendly face, modest but too welcoming to hide itself from the passing traveller, and composed in an utterly satisfying arrangement of windows, door and roof which had taken two centuries to evolve, and was to be seen repeated with subtle variations all over the southern counties.

Above The great staircase at the Vyne, Hampshire, built for John Chute in 1770. Jane Austen came to know the house through her brother James's friendship with the Chute family.

Opposite The Vyne from across the lake. The portico was attached to the Tudor house by John Webb, the disciple of Inigo Jones, in 1654.

Ibthorpe House, north Hampshire, the prettiest of the smaller Georgian houses which Jane Austen knew, and one which she often visited. It was the home of her closest friends, Mary and Martha Lloyd. Mary married her brother James, and Martha, after Jane's death, married another of her brothers, Sir Francis Austen.

It was owned by the Lloyd family, with whom Jane had made close friends when they lived in the Deane rectory. Their intimacy was cemented when James Austen married Mary Lloyd in 1797 as his second wife. Jane first visited Ibthorpe in 1792 when she was only seventeen and many times thereafter, often staying for weeks. It was the period when she was beginning to write prolifically, and she carried her current work there as she did everywhere. Local people provided her with copy, like Mrs Stent, an indigent friend and lodger of the Lloyds, who may have suggested Mrs Allen in *Northanger Abbey*, who 'had neither beauty, genius, accomplishment, nor manner ... and would remark aloud on any topic like breaking her thread or hearing a carriage or seeing a speck on her gown'; or the over-attentive Debary sisters, daughters of the vicar, whom she named 'the endless Debaries'. In November 1800 she wrote to Cassandra, 'Three of the Miss Debaries called here this morning after my arrival, but I have not yet been able to return their civility. You know it is not an uncommon circumstance in this parish to have the road from Ibthorp (*sic*) to the Parsonage much dirtier and more impracticable for walking than the road from the Parsonage to Ibthorp.'

But the house and the Lloyds delighted her. It has a dozen rooms and an outhouse which a century later Dora Carrington, the painter, made into a studio, each cool and homely, fitted together like a three-dimensional jigsaw, tight, clean, neat, and little altered by new conveniences. The staircase and the panelling are exactly as she knew them. It is Longbourn, it is Hartfield, it is Barton Cottage, yet it is none of them. It is simply a manifestation of all she meant by the decency and joy of country life.

III

KENT, 'THE ONLY PLACE FOR HAPPINESS'

Jane Austen knew intimately two English counties, Hampshire and Kent, and it is with Hampshire that she will be primarily associated because she was born there, lived the greater part of her life in two of its villages, and died in Winchester. But Kent can claim a major share in her life and inspiration, giving her much happiness and material for her books. One of her brothers, Edward, inherited a great estate near Canterbury, and she was often his guest there for months on end. And it was in Kent that the Austen line originated. They were minor country gentry, deeply rooted in the land. Her own generation was even less genealogically minded than our own, thinking it a dismal and morbid science, and it is unlikely that Jane showed much interest in the successive clothiers, farmers, attorneys and surgeons whose memorials in Kentish churches bear the family name and from whom her father was directly descended. It is worth exploring, as she did not, this seed-bed of her genius.

Go then to a village near Cranbrook in the Weald of Kent called Horsmonden. It is a country of hops and orchards, wheat and sheep, quite thickly wooded but on the cleared land intensively cultivated and grazed, the green slopes barred by hedgerows and speckled with the brown and white of farmhouses and oasts. Its air of prosperity is due to the frequency of old manor houses, for this was not only good farming country but from the middle ages to the seventeenth century the centre of England's woollen and iron manufacture which moved to the Midlands in time to spare the South the excesses of the Industrial Revolution and leave behind these sturdy but graceful mansions built with the profits of the trade.

One of them is Grovehurst, the Austen house. They are known to have lived there since the reign of Queen Elizabeth. A John Austen heads the pedigree, and Johns II, III, IV, V, VI and VII succeed him with their brothers Francis, Thomas, William, Henry and so on, but it is almost always a John Austen who is the householder of Grovehurst and its near neighbour, Broadford, another Austen manor, until the last of them died in 1851. They started as wool-merchants and clothiers, ended as prosperous farmers, and Grovehurst itself is evidence of the stages in their rise. It is a superb example of the Wealden hall-house, some say two of them joined by a Tudor wing, and inside there is enough panelling, fireplaces, oak staircases, 'priest-holes' and capacious cupboards, with neighbouring rooms on different levels, to satisfy the most pertinacious of archaeologists and the dreamiest inventor of romantic legends.

Jane Austen may never have seen Grovehurst or even heard its name, because her branch of the family bifurcated from Horsmonden nearly a century before to become the Tonbridge-Sevenoaks Austens. Her first acquaintance with Kent was therefore with a great-uncle, Francis Austen, a prosperous solicitor who owned the large and beautiful town house in Sevenoaks called the Red House. It survives, still as a solicitor's office, near the entrance to Knole. She and Cassandra were taken there in 1788 when Jane was twelve and Francis ninety. He had built his career and fortune as Clerk of the Peace for Kent and on his private practice as a solicitor to local families like the 3rd Duke of Dorset, and by marrying two heiresses in succession. Jane called it 'ill-gotten wealth', but nobody else thought so. It had paid for the education of her father at Tonbridge School and St John's College, Oxford (where he won a scholarship), and bought him the living at Deane.

Previous page Godmersham, between Ashford and Canterbury, the home of Edward Austen which Jane Austen visited more often and for longer periods than any other house. If there is an original for Pemberley in *Pride and Prejudice*, it must be this. She knew the house when she wrote the first draft of the novel, and had become very familiar with it when she revised the draft for publication.

Grovehurst, near Cranbrook, Kent, where generations of Austens had lived and farmed. It is doubtful whether Jane Austen ever saw the house, but she would have appreciated its history and style, for though her taste was classical, she enjoyed the rambling sturdiness of manor-houses like Donwell Abbey in *Emma*.

The Red House, Sevenoaks, Kent, a fine example of a William and Mary town-house. Built in 1686, it was purchased in 1743 by Francis Austen, Jane's great-uncle, and in July 1788, aged 13, she stayed there for a month.

Following page Bifrons Park, Kent, a painting attributed to Jan Siberechts. It was a house near Canterbury belonging to Edward Taylor. In 1796 Jane wrote to her sister that she 'contemplated it with a melancholy pleasure, the abode of him [Taylor] on whom I once fondly doted'. The house was demolished in 1948.

Francis's son Francis Motley Austen succeeded him as Clerk of the Peace. Selling the Red House, he bought an even more imposing establishment just outside Sevenoaks called Kippington, where he brought up eleven children and entertained lavishly. The house is a striking example of the grander upper-middle class mansion of 1760, white, cool and dominant. Today it sails between the smart commuter houses like a yacht among a crowd of fishing smacks. It is possible that Jane saw it, but more interesting is the speculation that she walked across the park to Knole or visited Chevening on the far side of the town, either of which would have been her first sight of a house of the highest aristocratic and architectural rank. Our only record of her visit to Sevenoaks is not her own but her cousin's, Philadelphia Walter, who was meeting her for the first time and thought her 'whimsical and affected' and 'not at all pretty and very prim, unlike a girl of twelve', but then 'Phila' was a vain girl in her twenties and Jane was shy.

In her adult life it was with east Kent that she was more closely connected, passing through the north and west of the county quickly

Kippington, also in Sevenoaks, was the property of Francis Austen's son Francis Motley Austen, and the Austens held it for three generations. In 1801 Jane wrote that her father and brother Frank had postponed a visit there, and she would have had many opportunities to go there herself on her journeys from London to east Kent.

on her journeys direct from Hampshire or through London. Kent was then at its most prosperous and beautiful. 'It is the only place for happiness', she wrote: 'Everybody is rich there'. A glance at contemporary maps like Andrews' (1769) or the first Ordnance Survey sheets (1801) shows gentlemen's estates, large and small, overlapping each other like water-lily leaves on a pond. It was an aristocratic county, owing its affluence to its location between London and the Channel ports and the richness of its soil. Many of the larger houses remained for centuries in the hands of the same families. When you examine, in Harris's or Hasted's county histories, the engravings of these houses as they existed in Jane's day, you will see how neat even the smallest of them were, how tonsured their gardens and surrounding orchards. It may be an idealised picture, ignoring the terrible state of the minor roads and the decay of the dwellings of the poor, but looking at Jan Siberecht's painting of Bifrons (pages 58–9) which illustrates how beautifully a large manor house settled into the ancient landscape, one can understand the pleasure which Jane Austen took in returning again and again to her brother's neighbouring estate of Godmersham.

Edward Austen had not achieved his prosperity by effort, but by adoption and inheritance. He and his siblings had been brought up in genteel poverty, their father (though his children never knew it) often finding it necessary to appeal for loans to his richer relations to supplement his stipend. It was a struggle, for there were eight children, six boys and two girls. So it was without any sense of betrayal that the Rev. George, with Mrs Austen's strong encouragement, gave away his third son Edward to Thomas and Catherine Knight of Godmersham with whom they had a common ancestor in John Austen III who died in 1705. The Knights were childless, and forming an attachment to Edward in his boyhood, proposed the adoption in 1783 when he was sixteen. The scene is deliciously depicted in William Wellings' silhouette reproduced on page 62. When his adoptive father died in 1794, he left his estates in Kent and Hampshire to his widow for life, with a reversion to Edward on her death. By 1797 Catherine Knight, anticipating the bequest, made over the estate to Edward and retired to Canterbury. He took the name of Knight when his adoptive mother died in 1812. So it came about that all his brothers and sisters, but specially Jane and Cassandra, enjoyed his generous hospitality throughout their adult lives, and Godmersham became for Jane the central architectural experience of her life.

But not immediately. In 1791, before his succession to the estate, Edward married Elizabeth Bridges, a daughter of Sir Brook Bridges of Goodnestone Park near Wingham, and their early married life was

Knole in the late eighteenth century by Hendrik de Cort, a drawing now at Sissinghurst Castle, Kent. This great house lay within easy walking distance from Francis Austen's in Sevenoaks, and as he was solicitor to the Duke of Dorset who owned it, it is highly likely that he took her there during her childhood visit to him in 1788. If so, it would have been her first acquaintance with a house of the first architectural rank.

spent in a house called Rowling, only a mile from the Park and belonging to it. The two houses were very significant in the development of Jane's taste and knowledge, for they were of different qualities, Rowling small and compact, Goodnestone moderately large and grand, and at the time when she knew them best, she was already engaged on the first versions of *Sense and Sensibility* and *Northanger Abbey*.

Goodnestone (pronounced 'Gunston') is an early eighteenth-century brick house, later heightened by the addition of an extra storey without spoiling its proportions, a difficult feat achieved by raising the pediment with it. It might be called severe and over-fenestrated (like more teeth than even a generous mouth can gracefully accommodate) but the pleasant marriage of brick and stone, the beauty of the garden and the elegance of the main rooms are wholly satisfying. There is no record that Jane Austen ever stayed a night there, but she often visited it from Rowling and at least once danced there. It was in September 1796:

We dined at Goodnestone [she wrote to Cassandra] and in the evening danced two country dances and the Boulangeries. I opened the ball with Edward Bridges; the other couples were Lewis Cage and Harriot [Bridges]; Frank [Jane's brother] and Louisa [Bridges]; Fanny and George [Cage]. Elizabeth Austen [née

A silhouette by William Wellings of George Austen (untypically dressed in tailcoat and silk stockings) presenting his son Edward to Thomas and Catherine Knight of Godmersham. The Knights adopted the boy and made him heir to their estates.

Rowling was a house near Canterbury belonging to the Bridges of Goodnestone, and Edward Austen lived there when he married Elizabeth Bridges in 1791. Jane Austen began the first versions of *Sense and Sensibility* and *Northanger Abbey* while she was staying with her brother and sister-in-law. The porch, the annex on the left and the bay on the right are later additions, but the 'Georgian goodness' of the main house is still apparent.

Bridges] played one Country Dance, Lady Bridges the other, which she made Henry [Jane's brother] dance with her; and Miss Finch played the Boulangeries ... We supped there and walked home at night under the shade of two umbrellas.

What an insight such letters give us on contemporary manners! All the people mentioned except Miss Finch were related by birth or marriage to the Bridges. So small and impromptu a dance could be called a ball. They provided their own music. Jane was asked, though only twenty, to open the ball with the son of the house, but when she left, she was made to walk, in the dark and in the rain, the mile back to Rowling. She accepts her ill-treatment without comment or resentment, but it was on such social subtleties of favour and neglect that she composed

Opposite Goodnestone House was originally two-storeys high but in the mid-eighteenth century an additional storey was added and the proportions of the façade restored by elevating the pediment to its present height.

Goodnestone Dower House, where Lady Bridges lived with her daughters in her widowhood. Though we do not know for certain that Jane Austen ever slept at Goodnestone House, she certainly spent nights in the Dower House, and her bedroom was probably that under the right-hand dormer window.

many situations in her early novels. She began *First Impressions* (the first version of *Pride and Prejudice*) as soon as she returned from this visit to Steventon.

During her widowhood Lady Bridges lived next door to the great house at what was then called Goodnestone Farm, now the Dower House, with her unmarried daughters and orphaned grand-daughters, the Cages. Jane stayed there for several nights in August 1805, making use of Lady Bridges's own bedroom where she found the shelves in a state of great disorder ('what a treat for my mother to arrange them!'), and from there walked round the park and revisited Rowling, 'and very great was my pleasure in going over the house and grounds'. For it was at Rowling that she had been happiest, staying there at least twice with Edward and Elizabeth until they moved to Godmersham, busy with her writing, her needlework, the piano, amusing their young children, walking, and visiting the coast which was so close that one could see the sea from the attic windows. The Georgian goodness of the house shines through its later additions. It was subject to constant 'improvements' like Woodston Parsonage in *Northanger Abbey*, 'a new-built substantial stone house, with its semi-circular sweep and green gates' of which General Tilney condescendingly says, 'a mere Parson-

age, small and confined we allow, but decent perhaps and habitable, and altogether not inferior to the generality. It may admit of improvement, however, anything in reason – a bow thrown out perhaps', as one was at Rowling, not to its disadvantage.

Godmersham, too, is changed, and at the time of this writing it is empty, undergoing a major refit, like a battleship. The rooms will soon be reinvigorated, and the house has been preserved as one of the loveliest in Kent to survive from the early part of the eighteenth century. The architect is unknown, but of the school of the Palladian architect Roger Morris, and he took every advantage of its site, which lies fairly low in the broad valley of the Stour between Wye and Chilham, looking north to the Pilgrims Way and south across the river to a long ridge of the Downs. 'Every disposition of the ground was good; and she looked on the whole scene, the river, the trees scattered on its banks and the winding of the valley, with delight'. This was Pemberley in *Pride and Prejudice*, and Pemberley was in Derbyshire, but Jane had only to lift her eyes to her Godmersham window to see what she was describing.

In her lifetime the improvements were true improvements. The flanking pavilions were added in 1785, and the road from Ashford to

Godmersham in the late eighteenth century. From Edward Hasted; *History of the County of Kent*, 1799.

Canterbury which ran directly past the house was switched to the river's far bank. Edward made considerable changes to the interior when he took over the estate. One gets from Jane's letters a good idea of its spaciousness, the bonus of privacy won from its many rooms: the breakfast parlour, library ('where we live, except at meals'), the dining-room, the drawing-room, billiards room, and upstairs the Yellow Room, the Chintz Room ('which I admire very much'), all of them centred on the hall with its stone floor inset with black marble squares, its *oeil-de-boeuf* windows and elaborate doorways and overmantel, the whole finished with a controlled richness of plasterwork. From her descriptions one can identify the main downstairs rooms, though the bedroom floor has been reconstructed since her day:

> Our two brothers [Edward and James] were walking before the house as we approached, as natural as life. Fanny and Lizzy [two of Edward's children] met us in the Hall with a great deal of pleasant joy; we went for a few minutes into the breakfast parlour, and then proceeded to our rooms. Mary [James Austen's wife] has the Hall chamber. I am in the Yellow Room – very literally – for I am writing in it at this moment. It seems odd to me to have such a great place all to myself. (To Cassandra, 15 June 1808.)

One of Jane's nieces, Marianne Knight, recalled in old age:

Family life in late eighteenth-century England, by John Harden.

Opposite left Edward Austen, Jane's brother, whose adoption by the Knights is illustrated by the silhouette on page 62, lived at Godmersham for the rest of his life and became the wealthiest of the Austen family, inheriting not only the Godmersham estates but the Steventon and Chawton properties in Hampshire as well.

Opposite right The fireplace in the hall at Godmersham surmounted by a stucco relief of Romans sacrificing at an altar. The plasterwork is of excellent quality, contemporary with William Kent's work on neighbouring houses like Mereworth.

Opposite below The garden-front at Godmersham.

Following page The temple overlooking Godmersham park, where Jane Austen is said (inevitably, but without proof) to have written some chapters of *Pride and Prejudice*. It is in *Sense and Sensibility* that she refers to a 'Grecian temple' at Cleveland, from where 'her eye, wandering over a wide tract of country to the south-east, could fondly rest on the farthest ridge of hills', as it could from here.

I remember that when Aunt Jane came to us at Godmersham she used to bring the manuscript of whatever novel she was writing with her, and would shut herself up with my elder sisters in one of the bedrooms to read them aloud. I and the younger ones used to hear peals of laughter through the door, and thought it very hard that we should be shut out from what was so delightful ... I also remember [she added] how Aunt Jane would sit quietly working [which meant sewing] beside the fire in the library, saying nothing for a good while, and then would suddenly burst out laughing, jump up and run across the room to a table where pens and paper were lying, write something down, and then come back across to the fire and go on quietly working as before.

That was the domestic scene. But Godmersham was also a centre of local society, a sort of jollier Vyne, to which visitors came almost daily, often without notice, and there was always a chaise available in the stables to take the residents on return visits. It was a rather wider society than Steventon's: fewer lords but more baronets, and a crowd of gentry living in unrepentant idleness. Below their level were the houses of the indigent or elderly, like Eggarton House on the opposite side of the river to Godmersham, where the two Miss Cuthberts cared for Thomas Knight's weak-minded sister to whom Jane paid charitable visits; or Standen, near Biddenden, one of the many farms on the Godmersham estate, tenanted by the Day family from 1727 to 1873, once a lovely Elizabethan manor house, now defaced, which could be made lovely again by restoring its windows and refurnishing its panelled rooms. Neither was the sort of place to provide Jane Austen with copy. She did not write about the insane, and only once about a farmer like the Days': Robert Martin in *Emma*. She preferred the elegant or the slightly dotty, like Miss Milles of Nackington, 'who undertook in *three words* to give us the history of Mrs Scudamore's reconciliation, and then talked on about it for half-an-hour', just like Miss Bates; or Mrs Britton, 'a large ungenteel woman, with self-satisfied and would-be elegant manners'. There were many such people in a neighbourhood where there was little else for the gentry to do but talk.

The greater houses spread fanlike from Godmersham towards Canterbury and Wye. Nearest to it, a walk away, was Chilham Castle, the two estates marching together bordered by the Stour. The house is a strange and beautiful Jacobean hexagon missing its sixth side to form an open courtyard, and the garden falls away in terraces towards the river and a 'Capability' Brown park. Cassandra and Jane were frequent guests at James Wildman's dinners and balls, but the Chilham occasion

of which she wrote most memorably was a dinner party in November 1813 which numbered 'only 14'. 'I must leave off being young. I find many Douceurs in being a sort of Chaperon, for I am put on the sofa near the fire and can drink as much wine as I like.' She was within a month of her thirty-eighth birthday, and had just finished writing *Mansfield Park*. There was music that evening to which Mr Wildman 'listened or pretended to listen', and next day the whole party drove to Canterbury for a concert which left Jane so tired 'that I began to wonder how I should get through the Ball next Thursday'. The ball was to be at Godmersham. With such entertainments they filled their days, depending on a corps of servants to feed, cosset and transport them. At Godmersham alone there were fourteen.

It is only if she happened to mention them in letters that we know which houses Jane frequented, and as she was writing from Rowling or Godmersham mainly to her sister, she took for granted everything that Cassandra would know, which family belonged to which house, or a house at which they called so often that another visit was barely worth mentioning. Did she, for example, ever see Olantigh or Knowlton Court or Bettshanger, or Broome Park (the most original seventeenth-century house in England) or lovely Bourne Place? We know that she attended balls at Ramsgate and Ashford, and even went prison-visiting in Can-

Above Chilham Castle, a Jacobean house with a 'Capability' Brown garden and park, within walking distance of Godmersham.

Opposite Knowlton Court, the imposing mansion of Sir Narborough D'Aeth, a neighbour of the Bridges of Goodnestone. Kent was a mosaic of contiguous estates of this kind, and Jane's not wholly cynical remark that the county 'is the only place for happiness, as everybody is rich there' was well deserved. From John Harris's *History of Kent*, 1719.

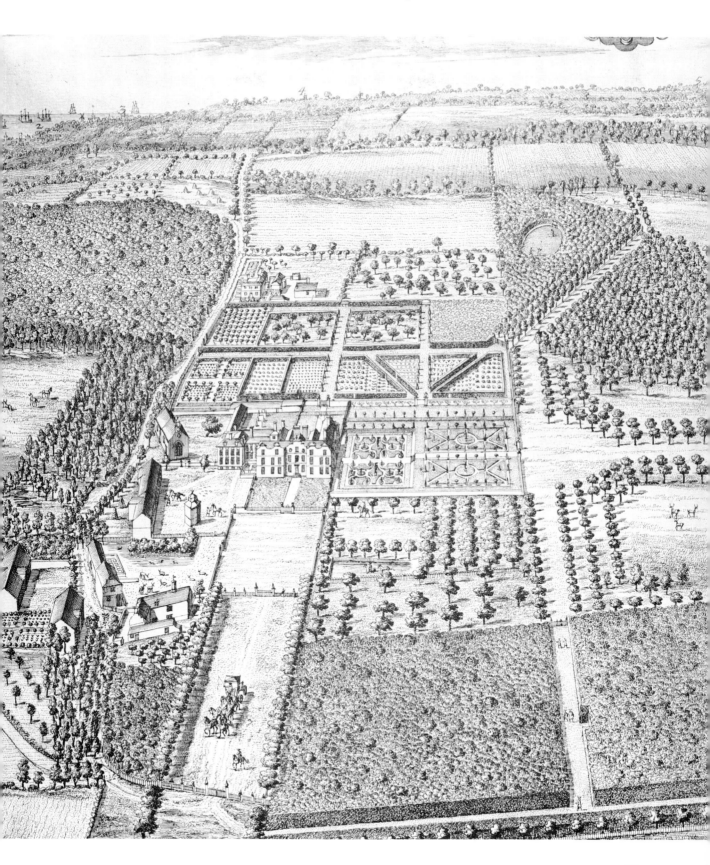

terbury, but what were her impressions of its cathedral, and did she ever see delectable Sandwich, or Tunbridge Wells at the peak of its popularity, or pretty Maidstone before it was Victorianised?

Chance references that such-and-such a person was met at such-and-such a party is often our only clue that the Austens knew the family and may have visited them at home. For instance, the Tokes of Godinton, an imposing Stuart mansion reclining delicately on its park, and inside gleaming with carved and polished oak in a succession of intimate rooms. Did Jane ever see it? She never specifically says she did, but from several affectionate references to the family ('as for Mr Toke there are few people whom I like better'; 'Mr Toke I am always very fond of'), it seems probable that she was sometimes their guest, and sitting in one of its many alcoves and window seats, or mounting its gnarled staircase, I need little persuading that my hand is resting where hers rested too.

Then there is Mersham-le-Hatch, the only Robert Adam house which she knew, a poor example of his artistry, as his patron, Sir Wyndham Knatchbull, messed up his design, his first on returning from Italy in 1762. The house is doubly connected by marriage to the

Godinton Park, near Ashford, for four centuries the home of the Toke family for whom Jane Austen cherished a particular affection. It is typical of the larger Kent houses to which she would have gone as her brother's guest.

74

Austens. Thomas Knight's wife was born a Knatchbull, and Edward's daughter Fanny married Sir Edward Knatchbull in 1820. From their union descended the Lord Brabournes who still own the house. It is of red brick with stone dressings, square pavilions flanking the main block, conventional, a bit dull, and although there is no certainty that Jane ever went there, her nicely familiar abbreviation of the name to 'Hatch' suggests that she may have known it quite well.

We are on firmer ground with Sandling, 'Mr Deedes' new house', ten miles from Ashford on the Folkestone road, where for once an architectural detail aroused her interest, a window placed exactly over a fireplace, which cannot now be checked as Sandling was flattened by a bomb in 1940. She was there in 1805, and probably again in 1813 for a day and a night, for William Deedes and his wife Sophie were very pressing. In such ways were links formed with the leading families of Kent below the ducal level, but these friendships seem never to have reached the degree of intimacy which the Austens enjoyed with some of the Hampshire families. Research has not discovered a single letter from Jane Austen to anyone in Kent but members of her own family, as if these Kentish acquaintanceships were regarded by both sides as agreeably superficial and terminable.

It was thus with the family of Rev. Sir John Fagg of Mystole, an imposing brick cube of a house near Godmersham which Jane, to her and our surprise, found 'so pretty', when prettiness is the last epithet one would apply to its sturdy stateliness. Her reception there in 1813 is typical of many such encounters:

The Ladies were at home: I was in luck and saw Lady Fagg and all her five daughters, with an old Mrs Hamilton from Canterbury and Mr and Mrs Chapman from Margate into the bargain. I never saw so plain a family, five sisters so very plain! ... Fanny did her part very well, but there was a lack of talk altogether, and the three friends only sat and looked at us.

Following page Mersham-le-Hatch, the only Robert Adam house which Jane Austen knew, was the childhood home of Catherine Knight of Godmersham, and later of Fanny Knight, Edward's daughter, after her marriage to Sir Edward Knatchbull. From Edward Hasted's *History of the County of Kent*, 1799.

So it must have been, in one smart house after another, the 'ladies' palely waiting for visitors and grimly smiling when they came, discussing (if they spoke at all) other ladies, other visits, and saving their spicier remarks for when the family was once more left alone.

Passing Bifrons, near Patrixbourne, in 1796 when she was not yet twenty-one, Jane 'contemplated with a melancholy pleasure the abode of him on whom I once fondly doted'. This was Edward Taylor, whose 'beautiful dark eyes' she still remembered four years later. Of the house she says nothing, but it was an exceptionally lovely place (see the

Siberecht painting, page 58–9), built originally in 1600, extended in 1694, and rebuilt by the Taylors in 1767 as an elegant Georgian house on three floors. It suffered another major rebuilding in 1864 which effectively destroyed the house which Jane knew. Even this latest Bifrons is lost to us. It was pulled down in 1948.

Eastwell Park has a special significance because like Laverstoke in Hampshire it was a new house designed by the Italian immigrant, Joseph Bonomi, who is mentioned, not favourably, in *Sense and Sensibility*. Lying between Godmersham and Ashford it was the third house on its site, and was finished for George Finch-Hatton in 1799 in a style quite alien to the English tradition, classical but defying classical rules by an immense arched portico on which Jane may have based her poor opinion of his work. She dined there in 1805, quite pleasantly ('they were very civil to me, as they always are', implying earlier visits), although Lady Elizabeth Finch-Hatton, George's wife, had astonishingly little to say for herself, and her daughter not much more. When they returned a call to Godmersham, 'they came and they sat and they went'. The house was totally rebuilt in 1926 and is now a very smart hotel.

This ends, though it cannot complete, the list of houses in east Kent which Jane Austen came to know during her long visits to her brother

Mystole House, between Godmersham and Canterbury, the home of the Rev. Sir John Fagg and his unappetising daughters whom Jane visited with little pleasure. The front with bay windows was added in 1895 to the original Georgian house on the right.

Eastwell Park, designed for the Finch-Hattons by Joseph Bonomi, and built during the period of Jane's visits to her brother. She did not approve of its architect, and found the family civil but silent, so they played cribbage to avoid the need for conversation. From W. H. Ireland's *History of Kent*, 1829.

between 1794 and 1813. 'Are you pleased with Kent?', Darcy asks Elizabeth Bennet early in their prickly relationship. She was definitely pleased, and so was Jane. Tedious though she found many of the social obligations that her brother imposed on her, she endured them for his sake, and because she found some young men attractive and was skilled in the art of higher flirtation. She loved Edward dearly, and his family increasingly as it increased, making a favourite of Fanny, later Lady Knatchbull. She loved the luxury of Godmersham, its good food, its services and the privacy for writing that she never knew in any of her parents' homes. Above all she loved its countryside which in Kent is nowhere more beautiful than where the Stour breaks through the North Downs towards Canterbury, with woods and pastures and tenderly sited farmhouses and mansions, where everyone seemed perennially at peace with each other and the external world, even when the poor were suffering cruelly and Buonaparte was gathering his armies at Boulogne. It gave Jane Austen an experience from which she selected only the most pleasing aspect, for that was how she chose to view the world.

I add London to Kent's chapter for the contrast it provides, because Jane Austen usually passed through the capital on her way to and from Godmersham and stayed there a night or more. She was determined

79

not to like London, a prejudice she inherited from her mother. 'T'is a sad place', said Mrs Austen in 1770, 'I would not live in it on any account. One has not time to do one's duty either to God or to man.' Similar sentiments are echoed in her daughter's correspondence and novels. As early as 1796, she is found writing to her sister from Cork Street, Mayfair, 'Here I am once more in this scene of dissipation and vice, and I begin already to find my morals corrupted'. In her earliest polished work, *Lady Susan*, she drew a picture of urban greed, deceit and depravity in contrast to the supposed virtues inbred by country life. London is noisy, smokey, filthy. You can barely walk the streets without falling down an uncovered manhole or colliding with a bucket of nightsoil being removed through someone's front door. So much for Mayfair. The City was even worse. 'Mr Darcy may perhaps have *heard* of such a place as Gracechurch Street [where the respectable Gardiners lived], but he would hardly think a month's ablution enough to cleanse him from its impurities.' Her portrait of Eliza, Colonel Brandon's adoptive sister in *Sense and Sensibility*, left destitute and friendless in the East End, is the most harrowing she ever depicted.

She exaggerates. At the turn of the eighteenth century, London was a city of beautiful streets and houses, like Mrs Jennings's off Portman

Portman Square, London. Jane's brother Henry, who had married his widowed cousin Eliza de Feuillide (her first husband was guillotined), lived in some style in Upper Berkeley Street, just off the square, and when Jane visited them, she was in the centre of the fashionable district. She made it the London house of Mrs Jennings and the Dashwood sisters in *Sense and Sensibility*.

Square where the Dashwood sisters stayed, and Jane, when she forgot to abuse it, enjoyed it greatly – shopping, strolling, visiting exhibitions and the theatre, its parks and places of congregation, for in short bursts she did not particularly mind crowds. After a visit to the Liverpool Museum and the British Gallery she wrote to Cassandra, 'I had some amusement at each, although my preference for men and women always inclines me to attend more to the company than the sight'. There is an air of half-guilty excitement about her London letters, stimulated by the jovial companionship of her brother Henry and his second wife Eliza de Feuillide. London was not too oppressive. It was a large town but a small metropolis. Belgravia was pastureland and Paddington a village. Jane spoke of 'walking into London' from Sloane Street to do her shopping. She never stayed long enough to hate it, and her disapproval was half-mocking, expressed more in the novels than in real life.

On their earlier visits the Austens stayed in a hotel in Cork Street, probably the Bristol, close to the point where passengers joined or left the West Country coaches, and later Jane lodged with her brother Henry in the various houses he owned or rented as his affluence grew or waned. Most are lost to us. London is not Bath. 64 Sloane Street was totally rebuilt. So was 23 Hans Place, but the buildings that replaced Henry Holland's lovely crescent carry a plaque which illustrates Jane Austen's extraordinary fame, for all it says is that on this

The plaque on the site of 23 Hans Place, off Sloane Street. Jane stayed there with her brother only for a month or two at a time, and was delighted by it. It was here that she corrected the proofs of *Emma*, and received from the Prince Regent an invitation to dedicate it to him.

JANE AUSTEN NOVELIST STAYED WITH HER BROTHER HENRY IN A HOUSE ON THIS SITE 1814–1815

site a house once stood which belonged for a short period to her brother with whom she would stay from time to time. But the house did have some significance for her. It was here that she worked on the second edition of *Mansfield Park*, corrected the proofs of *Emma*, wrote part of *Persuasion*, and received from the Prince Regent's librarian the extraordinary suggestion that her next book should be an historical romance about the House of Coburg. She loved Hans Place, probably because it was then half in the country: 'It is a delightful place – more than answers my expectations . . . I find more space and comfort in the rooms than I had supposed, and the garden is quite a love.'

The only one of Henry's London houses to survive is 10 Henrietta Street, off Covent Garden, where he lived for a time above his bank before it went broke. The most one can say of it is that it exists, having undergone various transformations into offices and shops, and that she might have recognised a few enclosed spaces in the vicinity, like the garden of St Paul's church or the little alley, Goodwin's Court, which Anne-Marie Edwards discerned as the nearest in feeling to the whole of this district two centuries ago.

One regrets that Jane described London so sparsely. If she had looked on the curve of the Thames or the sweep of the tall narrow houses with the same benevolence that she bestowed on landscape, there would have been some hint of it in the London episodes of her books. There is no such hint. Like most country-dwellers she regarded London as a threatening presence, an evil allurement, which was surprisingly enjoyable when one was actually there, but in prospect and retrospect an abomination.

No. 10 Henrietta Street, now Rohan's shop, where Henry Austen had rooms above his bank, ample enough to lodge his sister and three nieces in 1813 when Jane broke her journey to Godmersham. She pronounced it, inspite of the squash, 'very comfortable'.

IV

AN INTERLUDE IN BATH

Bath: there is no town in England where one can better enjoy the eighteenth-century experience. It was created, or recreated, as an entity within only eighty years, 1720–1800, and has since been preserved almost untarnished because it is beautiful and its golden ashlar stone is enduring. Its grace and convenience, or as Jane Austen would say, its civility, are as pleasing today as then. Bath has a serenity which induces serenity in its most argumentative visitor.

The city was born when the elder John Wood and his son created order out of chaos in the medieval jungle of twisted streets round the 'baths' quarter, and built beyond the ancient walls and up the hillside a pattern of squares, circuses and crescents for the transient and resident gentry. It has something of the exhilaration of a theatre. The detail is even more enticing. The stone is creamy, silky. It cuts beautifully. The masons did their job so well that there is still pleasure in running a finger along the thin line where one block was laid upon another two hundred and fifty years ago. The tall, pale, identical houses, ranged straight or on a curve, form streets expressive of private satisfaction and communal bliss. Even the street-names cut into the stone of corner houses are the originals. And when you examine how this effect of urbanity is achieved, you discover that it is by the simple repetition of a simple but carefully calculated formula – rectangular holes cut into an oblong to make windows and a door. That is the face which every house presents to the street, all the more pleasing in sunlight when the shallow pediments and cornices cast shadows against the pale stone. When one house is joined on either side by another and another of exactly the same proportions, even if lifted or dropped a little to allow for the gradient of the street, it creates a rhythmic harmony which never ceases to delight the eye. When the pattern is elaborated by pilasters or raised, as is often the case, on basements, and the parade of houses is shaped into an arc, a complete circle, or an octagon like Laura Place, the effect is so seductive that even Robert Adam's Pulteney

Bridge looks cumbersome in comparison. The splendid uniformity of Bath's standard streets and their sudden transformation into crescents cut into the hillside as if by strokes of a scythe, all of them facing south to catch the sun, gave the city a Roman, almost an imperial distinction without loss of domesticity. The official Guide for 1800 scarcely exaggerates when it claimed that Bath had become 'one of the *most agreeable* as well as the *most polite* places in the Kingdom, owing chiefly to the elegant neatness of its buildings and the accommodation for strangers, which are superior to those of any city in Europe'.

It was a place for walking. Ever since Beau Nash's arrival there in 1705, decency, order and cleanliness were Bath's accepted rules. He insisted that the streets should be clean and paved, the lodgings neat, the insolence of the chairmen and link-boys curbed. Most Palladian architecture aimed to make you feel grand: Bath's aimed to make you feel decorous and safe. The pavements on either side of the streets were wide and level, as smooth as the house-fronts laid flat, and when the fall of the ground made variation necessary, it was by shallow steps and raised walkways guarded on the outer side by railings. Some alleys were pedestrianised, and to this day have never been crossed by wheels. But in the older part of the town, around the Pump Room, there

Previous page Sydney Gardens in 1805 by J. C. Nattes. The house was built as a hotel (now a museum) almost directly opposite the Austens' house in Sydney Place. Behind it were extensive pleasure grounds, now crossed by the Avon canal and Brunel's railway.

Opposite The Circus (north segment) as it was in 1784, by Thomas Malton. The façades and the railings round the basements are unchanged since then, but in the centre of the Circus great plane trees now mar the scale of the buildings and interrupt the vistas from the three streets that lead into it.

Right The central house in Camden Crescent, designed by John Eveleigh in 1788 on the slopes of Beacon Hill overlooking Bath. It was in this grand crescent (then named Camden Place), and perhaps in this very house, that Jane Austen lodged the vain Sir Walter Elliot in *Persuasion*.

Queen Square, which was John Wood's first great undertaking in Bath, begun in 1729. The whole north side was designed as the wing of a vast country mansion of which one corner is shown opposite. Facing it across the square were more modest buildings, in one of which, No. 13 (*right*), the Austens lodged during their first extended visit to the city in 1799.

must have been a considerable bustle of carriages where cars are now prohibited. One recalls the scene in *Persuasion*:

> Coming opposite to Union Passage . . . they were prevented crossing by the approach of a gig, driven along a bad pavement by a most knowing-looking coachman with all the vehemence that could most fitly endanger the lives of himself, his companion and his horse.

It was an area of the city so complex in plan that it was the perfect setting (as if in a Restoration Comedy) for brief encounter and quick avoidance, the glimpse of a friend through one archway or escape from an enemy through another. Jane Austen made clever use of it in her novels.

Bath as we know it was a relatively new city when the Austens stayed there, first for a month or two in 1797 and 1799, and then for four years after they left Steventon in 1801. Beechen Cliff had limited expansion to the south, and the low ground beside the River Avon where now modern buildings attempt unsuccessfully to compliment the Georgian without exactly imitating them, was considered unhealthy for the valetudinarians whom the city hoped to attract. The alternative was to build northwards up a fairly steep hillside which would benefit the chair-carriers more than their elderly passengers, or on the opposite side of the Avon where the Austens eventually decided to settle. The Circus was completed in 1758, the Royal Crescent in 1774, Lansdowne Crescent in 1793, Camden Crescent in the next year, but Pulteney Street and Laura Place were not finished until 1795, only two years before the Austens' first visit. A thousand houses were added in the 1790s, and Jane Austen had the experience of living in quite a number of them.

In 1799 they took lodgings for six weeks on the south side of Queen Square, at the corner of Prince's Street. The square was John Wood's first bold experiment to create a row of houses in the form of a wing of a very large country house, uniting them by columns and a central pediment. The west side of the square was not enclosed as it is today by a continuous line of buildings but by two town houses of elegant but not monumental size separated by their gardens. No. 13, the Austen house, is on the cheaper side, facing north. It is still a handsome house, surprisingly large and smart to be rented by so impecunious a family.

> We are exceedingly pleased with it [wrote Jane to Cassandra, who was joining them later]. The rooms are quite as large as we expected. Mrs Bromley [landlady] is a fat woman in mourning, and

No. 1 The Paragon belonged to Mrs Austen's brother, and it was the temporary lodging of the family while they were searching for a house of their own in 1801. It is one of a thousand such houses which repeat, with subtle variations, the pattern of door and windows inset in the creamy Bath stone, making the city the loveliest architectural legacy of eighteenth-century England.

The doorway of 4 Sydney Place, the Austens' house from 1801 till 1804. It is the only house in Bath, out of the six (all surviving) which they inhabited at various times, to bear a tablet in Jane's memory.

a little black kitten runs about the staircase ... I like the situation very much; it is far more cheerful than The Paragon, and the prospect from the drawing-room window, at which I now write, is rather picturesque, as it commands a perspective view of the left side of Brock Street, broken by three Lombardy poplars in the garden of the last house in Queen's Parade.

Nice landlady, nice kitten, nice view, but typically she notices the three poplars rather than John Wood's masterpiece across the square (its façade was then unimpeded by trees), for Jane was not taken with Bath's architecture, only with its shops and pleasant accommodation. There is only one passage in her surviving letters and the two Bath novels, *Northanger Abbey* and *Persuasion*, to suggest that she found the city beautiful, and that was when Henry Tilney escorts his sister and Catherine Morland to the top of Beechen Cliff and lectures them on the picturesque, but pays so little attention to the lovely urban scene below them that Catherine 'voluntarily rejected the whole city of Bath as unworthy to make part of a landscape.'

The Paragon which she mentioned in her letter about Queen Square was a house belonging to James Leigh Perrot, Mrs Austen's wealthy brother. They had stayed there on their first visit in 1797, and when they moved to Bath in 1801, it was again their temporary lodging while they went house-hunting. No. 1 The Paragon was the first in a row of houses built by Thomas Atwood in 1770, unusual in that the windows of its rear side were ranged as carefully as on the front, but awkward as a residence because it faced the city's busiest and steepest road from which it is protected by one of those elevated walks that form so pleasing a feature of the city.

After searching many parts of Bath for a suitable house and rejecting several for their expense or suspected dampness (Jane called them 'putrefying'), the Austens finally settled on No. 4 Sydney Place. It was an excellent choice. The row had been built in 1792 by Thomas Baldwin as a modest extension of his magnificent parade, Pulteney Street, and lay opposite Sydney Gardens, large pleasure grounds laid out in 1795 to include bowling greens, artificial waterfalls, a labyrinth, stages for fireworks and outdoor concerts, two iron bridges built over the Avon Canal, and the Sydney Hotel, now the Holbourne of Menstrie Museum, built in 1796 like a country mansion. Bath stopped at this point. No Georgian estate was erected beyond it. The countryside was immediately available, and a fifteen-minute walk would take you to the city centre. No. 4 Sydney Place, which was Jane's home for the next three years, is, for Bath, an undistinguished building though it retains the smooth masonry and decency of line which Baldwin inherited from the Woods. Its occupants today understandably do not welcome the intrusion of strangers attracted by the plaque beside the front door which records Jane's residence there, but there is a description of its interior by Constance Hill who was allowed inside in 1901, exactly a hundred years after the Austens moved in:

> We sat in the pretty drawing-room with its three tall windows overlooking the Gardens. The morning sun was streaming in at these windows and falling upon the quaint empire furniture which pleasantly suggests the Austens' sojourn there. The house is roomy and commodious. Beneath the drawing-room, which is on the first floor, are the dining-room and arched hall from which a passage leads to a garden at the back of the house. The large old-fashioned kitchen, with its shining copper pans and its dresser laden with fine old china, looked as if it had remained untouched since the Austens' day.

Having signed the contract they went on holiday to Devon while the house was redecorated and newly furnished, since everything they owned, including George Austen's library and Jane's pianoforte, was unaccountably sold when they left Steventon. It made a house more than adequate for a family now reduced to Mr and Mrs Austen and their two daughters, and they lived there comfortably with a cook, housemaid and manservant on six hundred pounds a year.

Then in 1804 they moved to No. 27 Green Park Buildings, a larger house but less expensive, in the unfashionable area near the river. There George Austen died in January 1805, aged seventy-three, and was buried in the church where he had been married forty years earlier, St Swithin's, a Georgian church in Walcot Street. Twice more they moved for short periods, first to Gay Street, where Mrs Thrale lived and died, and finally Trim Street, making in Bath six 'Austen' houses, all of which survive externally unaltered.

It is puzzling why Jane Austen was unhappy there, and why she wrote nothing during those four years except her unfinished novel *The Watsons*. She had nothing much else to do, a comfortable house in which to write, and in the teeming society of Bath much to write about. But these were barren years. One explanation is that she was depressed by the publisher's rejection of *Pride and Prejudice* in 1797, the non-publication (though it was bought in 1803 by Crosby & Co for ten pounds) of *Northanger Abbey*, and her dissatisfaction with *The Watsons*. She may have thought that if she had ever had a gift for writing, it had

27 Green Park Buildings (the paler of the three houses here illustrated) was the Austen house in 1804–5, where Jane's father died in January 1805. Although it was in the newest and least fashionable part of Bath, the houses lost nothing in elegance and formed one side of a pleasant triangular green.

deserted her. It is not arguable that she hated Bath so much that she lived under a cloud of depression so thick and permanent that she had no inclination to seek refuge from it by her pen. She liked Bath, enjoyed its shops, theatre, dances and other amenities, her walks in its beautiful countryside, and to some extent its people, though she made no permanent friends there. Like Catherine Morland in *Northanger Abbey* she found there 'a variety of amusements, a variety of things to be seen and done all day long, which I can know nothing of there' – 'there' being the 'small, retired village' from which she came, like Steventon.

Northanger Abbey was written while Jane Austen was still in Hampshire and knew Bath only from visits of a few weeks each. *Persuasion* was written after living there for several years. The tone is not markedly different, given that Catherine Morland arrived in Bath in a state of high excitement and Anne Elliot unhappily, slighted by her father and sister and languishing from seven years of love for Captain Wentworth which she thought unrequited. In both novels there is a healthy acceptance that Bath is a place where snobs flourish, like Sir William Elliot who chose it because he thought he would shine there in contrast to the crowd of vulgar *arrivistes* and 'a man might be important at comparatively little expense'. But Jane could, and did, discover this attitude anywhere, not only in Bath, and the temptation to find in

After George Austen's death his widow and two daughters moved to Gay Street, a remarkably good neighbourhood for the now impoverished family. They moved once more before leaving Bath, to Trim Street, which is cramped, narrow and without architectural distinction.

Persuasion a reflection of her own loathing of the city should be resisted. It is true that there is a dearth of letters at this period by which one might judge the degree of her resentment, but knowing her sunny nature and her capacity for enjoyment, it is improbable that she spent much time moping while she was there. She had hated leaving Steventon because she had lived there all her life and her friends were there, and it was in the country. In fact, Sydney Place was so much on the outer fringe of Bath that it too was countrified, and it was simple for her to escape the 'white glare of Bath' of which Anne Elliot complained, without cause, for Bath stone does not glare like marble: it exudes a honey light. Missing Kellynch, Anne saw the city as hostile. Jane Austen had no particular wish to return to Steventon, which in any case she could often revisit as her brother James was now living in the Parsonage as the Rector.

She did not dislike crowds and could avoid them when she wished. She chose to patronise the Pump Room, which despite the throng of visitors Catherine Morland found 'admirably adapted for secret discourses and unlimited confidences', and the two Assembly Rooms, the Upper and the Lower. She often joined the fashionable strollers outside the Royal Crescent, even complaining once that 'it was not

The Pump Room, Bath, by J. C. Nattes. The statue of Beau Nash presides from the alcove, as it still does. This splendid room was not only the place where invalids drank the waters, but the centre of Bath's social gatherings.

crowded enough'. She jostled with the shoppers in Milsom Street, which a visitor early in the nineteenth century, Pierce Egan, described as 'all bustle and gaiety':

> Numerous dashing equipages passing and re-passing, others gracing the doors of the tradesmen, sprinkled here and there with the invalids in comfortable sedans and easy two-wheeled carriages [the so-called Bath Chair], all anxious to participate in this active part of Bath, giving a sort of finish to the scene.

In *Persuasion* Lady Russell makes her way through the congestion of people and traffic, and it is not an unsympathetic picture:

> Driving through the long concourse of streets from the Old Bridge to Camden Place, amidst the dash of other carriages, the heavy rumble of carts and drays, the bawling of newsmen, muffin-men and milkmen, and the ceaseless clink of pattens, she made no complaint. No, these were noises that belonged to the winter pleasures; her spirits rose under that influence; and like Mrs Musgrove she was feeling, though not saying, that after being long in the country, nothing could be so good for her as a little quiet cheerfulness.

And what peace the graceful streets of Bath could afford! One of the gentlest scenes in *Persuasion* is when Anne Elliot and Captain Wentworth rediscover their love, 'their spirits dancing in private rapture', and 'slowly paced the gradual ascent' from Union Street, through Queen Square, along the Gravel Walk to the Royal Crescent and upwards to Camden Place, heedless of passers-by, 'whether sauntering politicians, bustling housekeepers, flirting girls, nursery-maids and children' (from where in fact or in her imagination would those 'sauntering politicians' have emerged?), and there are few better examples of the use she makes of actual street-scenes to enhance a pleasure in companionship which she must have experienced herself to describe it so well.

She arranged her characters in Bath like chessmen on their appropriate squares, placing Sir Walter Elliot in Camden Place (now Camden Crescent) 'a lofty dignified situation, such as becomes a man of consequence'; Lady Dalrymple lower down the hill, but not in the social scale, in Laura Place, where the Austens would like to have lived if they could have afforded it, and rightly, because it is the most delicate of all Bath's *rond-points*; Admiral Croft in Gay Street; the Thorpes in Edgar Buildings in George Street; the Allens in Great Pulteney Street;

The Royal Crescent in 1784 by Thomas Malton. The nearest house, No. 1, has been redecorated and furnished in the best eighteenth-century taste, and is now on view to the public as a splendid illustration of the grander interiors familiar to us from the two Bath novels, *Persuasion* and *Northanger Abbey*.

and at the lowest level, socially and topographically, the impoverished widow Smith in Westgate Buildings. None of her characters is quite grand enough to inhabit the Circus or Royal Crescent, but she knew their interiors well enough to convey in her references to slightly less splendid apartments the luxury and beautiful finish of such rooms that one can recapture from the reconstruction of No. 1 Royal Crescent with its costly fabrics and tiptoe furniture. Jane was not given to eulogising such places. She took them for granted. Nor did she show any interest in the visual evidence of Bath's past history, for instance, the Roman baths which were first discovered under the Pump Room in 1755 and have been under almost constant excavation ever since, or, more surprisingly, the Abbey, one of the loveliest churches in England, where she must have attended many services. She never, it seems, drank Bath's famous waters, or bathed in them, preferring the Theatre Royal and the amusements staged in Sydney Gardens, just across the street from her house.

The Gardens were an attempt to reproduce on a provincial scale the attractions of Vauxhall in London. Extending over sixteen acres and bisected by the Kennet and Avon Canal which was still under construction in the 1800s, it was arranged in 'a great number of small delightful groves' according to the *New Bath Guide* of 1801, 'pleasant vistas, and charming lawns, intersected by serpentine walks, which at every turn meet with sweet, shady bowers furnished with handsome seats, some composed by nature, others by art', a design and a description which in all innocence marks the transition from classical sobriety to nineteenth-century romanticism. 'Four thatched umbrellas', the *Guide* helpfully adds, 'are placed at equal distances from each other, which are intended to serve as a shelter from sudden rains or storms.'

Jane Austen's other places of amusement were the Assembly Rooms. Her description in *Northanger Abbey* of Catherine Morland's first visit there when she and Mrs Allen knew nobody is conceivably based on

Bath Street, designed by Thomas Baldwin in 1791, one of the latest and most graceful of the Georgian streets which replaced the medieval complex in central Bath. A watercolour by Thomas Malton.

experience. 'She longed to dance, but she had not an acquaintance in the room.' This would have been the Upper Rooms, which were built near the new centre of Bath in 1769–71 to the design of John Wood the younger. The Lower Rooms on the North Parade, dating from 1708, were less frequented, but it was there that Catherine had better luck, being introduced to Henry Tilney by James King, the Master of Ceremonies whose real name Jane borrowed for the occasion. The old Rooms were finally demolished in 1933, but after a turbulent history, including massive damage in the Second World War, the Upper Rooms have been restored to their appearance when the Austens came to live permanently in Bath. Splendid as they were, they were not always well attended. Here is a description which well illustrates the contrast between the banality of real life and the drama of romance. It comes in a letter from Jane to Cassandra in May 1801:

> I dressed myself as well as I could, and had all my finery much admired at home. By nine o'clock my Uncle, Aunt and I entered the rooms and linked Miss Winstone on to us. Before tea it was rather a dull affair; but then the before-tea did not last long, for there was only one dance, danced by four couple. Think of four couple, surrounded by about a hundred people, dancing in the Upper Rooms at Bath! After tea we cheered up; the breaking up of private parties sent some scores more to the Ball, and though it was shockingly and inhumanly thin for this place, there were people enough I suppose to have made five or six very pretty Basingstoke assemblies.

Bath was losing its appeal for the eminent and well-born. There was a seepage and then a flood, of middle-class people attracted by its shops, hospitals and entertainments who could rent for a week or two furnished rooms which reminded them of home, with a difference. In the fifteen years that separated the writing of *Northanger Abbey* and *Persuasion*, Bath had gone down-market. Gone were the days when you could meet Addison, Nelson, Pitt, Fielding, Horace Walpole, Gainsborough or Herschel strolling up Milsom Street. Even for people like the Elliots the Rooms were no longer fashionable enough. They preferred to entertain at home, and while the young might go on to the Rooms as today they might visit a night-club after a dinner party, Sir Walter would only go there for concerts, having abandoned any expectation that he would find there even the consolation of a pretty face. It was the same with the Pump Room. Once it had attracted the élite of Bath more for the sake of seeing and being seen than for any medicinal properties of the waters, but now it was mainly resorted to by the elderly and sick from all over the country. The innumerable memorial tablets on the Abbey walls testify both to their presence and the inefficacy of the cure. The hypochondriacs as well as the genuinely sick like Mrs Smith gave the place a shabby reputation far removed from the sprightly respectability inspired by Beau Nash.

Bath should have been Jane Austen's ideal town. Its buildings, many of them spanking new when she first went to live there, were expressive of everything that she cared for – gentility, liveliness, reason, balance and a certain cumulative grace. She was comfortably housed with her parents and sister, and there was money enough to go on annual holidays to the seaside and to Kent. Her life was a round of mildly agreeable activity, and judging from the few of her letters that survive from the Bath period, she was not just content, but cheerful. Yet the two Bath novels leave behind an impression that life there was hectic and trivial, and that Jane, in expressing Anne Elliot's 'very determined, though very silent, disinclination for Bath' and her resignation to a long 'imprisonment' there, was hinting at her own feelings. If so, it could have been due to other causes than distaste for Bath itself, like her broken 'engagement' to Harris Bigg-Wither, her aborted romance on holiday at Sidmouth, disillusion with her writing, constant anxiety about her sailor brothers at an acute period of war (though both missed Trafalgar), the recurrent illnesses of Mrs Austen, the death of Mrs Lefroy, and hardest of all, the death of her own father a few weeks' later.

The family were left poor. Their income was now only two hundred pounds, but the sons supplemented it up to about six hundred pounds on which they lived for the remainder of Jane's life. They did not renew the lease of Green Park Buildings when it expired, moved temporarily to No. 25 Gay Street, then to the cheaper Trim Street, and in July 1806 left Bath for ever, 'with what happy feelings of escape', wrote Jane in a melancholy summing-up of the past five years.

They first went to Clifton, which she found more enjoyable than Bath because it was less busy, a residential suburb of Bristol, and architecturally distinguished for its fine Georgian terraces. In the early years of the new century the town was further expanded and embellished by Regency villas and terraces which Bath lacked. We do not know in which of the many lodging houses or private hotels the Austens stayed, but from her walks round the leafy suburbs Jane became familiar with the new style of balconied houses like those on Sion Hill, each distinct from its neighbour, unlike Bath's, but harmoniously linked by its gentle curve, or standing withdrawn from the street but overlooking

Sion Hill, a Regency terrace at Clifton, near the entrance to the later Clifton suspension bridge. The Austens moved to Clifton from Bath in 1806, but it is not known where they stayed.

it across a paved courtyard or garden as in Richmond Hill. In Jane Austen's novels Clifton appears as a watering-place recommended by Mrs Elton in *Emma*, and Blaise Castle is the object of John Thorpe's aborted expedition in *Northanger Abbey*. But there is nothing comparable to Fanny Burney's eulogy of Clifton in *Evelina*, where it figures as a spa where town and country meet on elegant terms. The Austens remained there but a short time before moving house once again, to Southampton.

V

THE COUNTRYSIDE

'The beauties of nature', wrote Jane Austen, 'must for me be one of the joys of heaven', and she meant the scenes with which she was most familiar, the friendly countryside of Hampshire and Kent. She knew no other type of landscape, perhaps thinking, like Catherine in *Northanger Abbey*, that Italy, Switzerland and the South of France must be 'fruitful in horrors'. As far as we know, she never saw a hill higher than the Cotswolds. The English lowland landscape was farmed to a visual perfection which we have not since recovered. The population of the whole of Britain in 1801 was only nine million, of whom one-fifth lived in towns, yet the land was as fully, if not as intensively, cultivated as it is today, the wars having made every acre of value for producing food. There was no waste land; the enclosures were more or less complete. Estate maps of the period show little deviation from modern maps in the pattern of hedgerows and small woods. The farm buildings were more attractive than ours – they used only indigenous materials like brick, tile, stone, timber and thatch – and in scale and colour they suited the environment, as if instinctively. The market towns were small and comely, and the villages pretty even when unclean.

Jane Austen's life coincided with the making of this landscape. Before starting to write *Mansfield Park* she asked Cassandra to find out whether there were yet hedgerows in Northamptonshire, so contemporary was the process of enclosing the common fields. She knew little of agriculture, though her father had farmed the glebeland at Steventon, and seems not to have cared much for animals except horses, but she rejoiced that the cultivation of land and the breeding of stock should have resulted in such a landscape, and gave credit for it not only to tenant-farmers like Robert Martin in *Emma*, but their landlords like Mr Knightley, and estate-owners like Sir Thomas Bertram whose first concern on returning to Mansfield Park from a year's absence abroad was to interview his steward and inspect his land. The farmland which pleased Jane the most was closely knit, wooded in moderation, neat and, above all, fecund, like Martin's farm, 'with all its appendages of prosperity and beauty, its rich pastures, spreading flocks, orchard in blossom, and light column of smoke ascending.'

Nobody enjoyed walking more than Jane. Throughout her life she would make a six-mile walk a feature of most days. At Steventon the opportunities had been restricted as the country was monotonous, but round Ibthorpe it swelled magnificently into hills that trailed oakwoods down to the valleys and the sloping meadows were spotted with gentle sheep. 'This, to my fancy', wrote William Cobbett, who knew Hurstbourne Tarrant well, 'is a very nice country. It is continual hill and dell.' Jane, with the Lloyd sisters, would climb the ridge behind the house and stride for miles beyond it with an exhilaration that is reflected in the pleasure that the Dashwood sisters took in similar country in *Sense and Sensibility*. When the Austens moved to Bath, its neighbourhood abounded in pleasant walks, like that to Charlcombe, 'sweetly situated

Previous page Lamberhurst, Kent. The eighteenth-century house on the left, Court Lodge, was the seat of William Morland, connected by marriage with Francis Austen of Sevenoaks. The relationship of the house to the church, set at a discreet distance from each other and both from the village, was quite a common arrangement in Jane Austen's novels.

A favourite Austen walk from Bath, the track across the fields to Charlcombe church.

in a little green valley, as a village with such a name ought to be', she wrote to Cassandra in 1799, having taken the existing path to the little Norman church where Henry Fielding, the author of *Tom Jones*, was married. Two years later she chose the opposite side of the Avon valley, through Lyncombe and Widcombe: 'For many, many yards together on a raised narrow footpath I led the way. The walk was very beautiful, as my companion agreed', she added with typical self-mockery, 'whenever I made the observation.'

Then there were journeys and round-trip expeditions by coach and carriage. The pace of travel was slow enough and the roads usually smooth enough for passengers to enjoy the changing scene, like Fanny Price on the expedition from Mansfield Park to Sotherton Court, 'observing the appearance of the country, the bearings of the roads, the differences of soil, the state of the harvest, the cottages, the cattle, the children', all of which indicate what Jane herself observed as she travelled the well-known road to London along the Hog's Back between Farnham and Guildford where 'there could not be a wood, or a meadow, or palace, or a remarkable spot in England that was not spread out before us on one side or the other.' In the same county, Surrey, was Box Hill, the destination of the famous seven-mile expedition in *Emma*. It is the summit of an unexpected cliff from which the view to the south across overlapping, caressing hills is still one of the most celebrated in southern England, marked with symbols of astonishment on tourist maps.

The villages are most changed. Dorking, so lovely a sight from Box Hill, turns out on closer inspection to be an unhappy example of the architectural damage done since 1800, and so is neighbouring Great Bookham where Jane was staying with her uncle, the Rev. Samuel Cooke, while writing part of *Emma*, and which, with greater plausibility than usual, can be taken as the model for Emma's Highbury, 'a large and populous village almost amounting to a town', but compact enough for every resident to know every other. Now no longer. The church, some shops brutally defaced, and a single street of workmen's houses are all that remains of 'Highbury'; not even the Rectory survives. The cross-roads in the centre of the village is a twentieth-century mess, and on the outskirts are closes, courts and dinky cul-de-sacs (telly inside, Mini outside), clean and eminently respectable but lacking the personality that only mystery can give. Great Bookham contains no mystery except how its past residents can have so ill-treated it.

One must not overpraise the Georgian village. Even Maria Bertram, anxious to show off Sotherton of which she was soon to become mistress, is obliged to admit that its cottages 'are really a disgrace', and in

Sanditon a cottage which seems from a distance neat and romantically situated is found to house a shepherd at one end and three old women at the other in conditions of rural squalor. Jane Austen knew such places. As her father's daughter she would visit them on charitable missions both at Steventon and Chawton, as did the haughty Lady Catherine de Bourgh 'whenever any of the cottagers were disposed to be quarrelsome, discontented or too poor'. But no scene in any of Jane's novels is set in the interior of a rustic cottage, there is no hint in them or in her letters that she was even aware of the misery the peasantry endured, no protest that the rich were getting richer as the poor grew poorer when rents and prices rose under the stress of war, and that the people were being reduced to a living standard lower than any since the Middle Ages, a condition so movingly described by Cobbett in *Rural Rides*. The upper section of society romanticised the lower to excuse the difference between them, and one of the symbols of that romanticism was the countryman's cottage, often depicted in prose and watercolour as rose-garlanded, thatched, sturdy, indestructible and charming, as a few of them were. Illustrated below and opposite are some of the survivors in different parts of the country that Jane knew well, but they cannot be called typical.

Cottages in different English counties, and made of different regional materials, which Jane Austen worked into the fabric of her books. *Below* at Farringdon, near Alton; *far right, below* at Adlestrop, near Stow-on-the-Wold, Gloucestershire; *far right, above* Crabtree Cottages, Surrey, on the way from Great Bookham to Box Hill, the expedition immortalised in *Emma*.

Bowood, Wiltshire. The temple and the lakeside cottage are features of the park which 'Capability' Brown modelled for the Marquess of Lansdowne in the 1760s. The temple is Doric, the cottage formerly the ferryman's. Together they perfectly illustrate two complimentary fashions in Jane's lifetime, the classic and the romantic.

Every property was subject to 'improvement', but none more so than the surroundings of the great house. Jane Austen was an expert on this. There had been improvements in every house that she had lived in, and her fictional houses would not be exceptions. To her the garden and the park were extensions of the house itself, and in *Pride and Prejudice* and *Mansfield Park* she analyses their qualities and capabilities. Pemberley, of course, was already too perfect to be further improved. Elizabeth Bennet

> admired every remarkable spot and point of view. They gradually ascended for half-a-mile, and then found themselves at the top of a considerable eminence where the wood ceased, and the eye was instantly caught by Pemberley House, situated on the opposite side of the valley, into which the road with some abruptness wound ... Elizabeth was delighted. She had never seen a place for which nature had done more, or where natural beauty had been so little counteracted by an awkward taste.

The park was ten miles round. Of course nature 'does most' everywhere in the country, but at Pemberley design and hard labour had made an important contribution. Jane is describing what in effect was a 'Capability' Brown park. There is no fussiness around the house. The flowers and vegetables, one imagines, are banished behind a distant enclosure. The view of the house from the park is as important as the view of the park from the house. Every clump of trees, each shining scimitar-curve of the river, contributes to a scene of Augustan placidity and aristocratic pride. Jane cannot help asking us to admire it, and she does it so obviously that she might be accused of making an error of taste, character and narrative by putting into Elizabeth's mind the temptation 'that to be mistress of Pemberley might be something!', when Elizabeth was determined to resist any further advances that Darcy might make to her. But it was more than the fantasy of becoming chatelaine of such a place. She was unwittingly attributing to Darcy the dignity, propriety and nobility of the scene before her. No man could create, or even inherit, such beauty without being worthy of it.

If Jane Austen had ever seen a 'Capability' Brown park in its prime, it might have been Bowood's in Wiltshire, for she could easily have visited it as a tourist on a journey between Hampshire and Bath. Brown had designed it in 1763 for the Marquess of Lansdowne. To achieve the result he wanted, it was necessary to remove an entire hamlet of which just one cottage remains, picturesquely posed on the far side of the lake. At Pemberley there was no lake, only a widening river, but

It is not proven that Jane Austen ever visited Bowood, which lay on her road from Hampshire to Bath, but there are few other places which reproduce so well the relationship between great house and placid lake that she imagines for Pemberley in *Pride and Prejudice*.

in other respects the scene is very similar – the woods, the curving drive, the shallow hills, the shorn grass and the distant view of a great stone house.

Sotherton was very different. It retained from the pre-Brown period the rigid formality of radiating avenues, and James Rushworth, who had inherited the estate with twelve thousand pounds a year, wanted to uproot them, for which he was reproached by Fanny Price and Edmund Bertram: 'Cut down an avenue!', says Fanny in a low voice, 'Does it not make you think of Cowper, "Ye fallen avenues, once more I mourn your fate unmerited"?' The last person of whom Rushworth was thinking was Cowper. He was thinking of Humphry Repton, and so was his fiancée: 'Your best friend upon such an occasion', says Maria, 'would be Mr Repton'. Jane Austen had seen at least one Repton garden. It was Adlestrop in Gloucestershire, the home of James-Henry Leigh, Mrs Austen's cousin, who in 1802 commissioned Repton to improve his estate:

a lively stream of water led through a flower garden, where its progress down a hill is occasionally obstructed by ledges of rock,

Adlestrop Park, Gloucestershire, which belonged to a cousin of the Austens who visited him there in 1806. It was designed by Sanderson Miller in the mid-eighteenth century and the garden was laid out by Humphry Repton. It was probably the only neo-Gothic house which Jane Austen knew at all intimately.

The countryside round Stow-on-the-Wold, Gloucestershire, looking towards
Adlestrop where Mrs Austen's cousin was vicar.

Opposite Stow-on-the-Wold from the terrace of Adlestrop Rectory (now Adlestrop
House), where the Austens stayed in 1806.

114

and after a variety of interesting circumstances it falls into a lake at a considerable distance, but in full view of the mansion and the parsonage, to each of which it makes a delightful, because a natural, feature of the landscape,

as Repton described it to his client in one of his Red Books. Adlestrop is perhaps one reason why Jane treated Repton in *Mansfield Park* with scant approbation. He was a destroyer of trees when Brown had been a planter, and he introduced artificial clutter round the house on a decreasingly small scale. He wanted to restore terraces, steps and balustrades which Brown had replaced by the lawn and the ha-ha, and to leave cornfields between the house and the distant view where Brown would only tolerate pasture. It was as if 'Pemberley' were suburbanised. But Jane did approve of Reptonian wildernesses round large country houses and shrubberies near small ones, like that at Hartfield where Mr Knightley proposed to Emma, and at Longbourn where the shrubbery was the scene of the strongest incident in all the novels, Elizabeth Bennet's refusal to yield to the bullying of Lady Catherine de Bourgh. The wilderness was a feature perhaps known to her from a childhood visit to Knole, and she makes use of it as a setting for a *Midsummer Night's Dream* series of encounters at Sotherton.

Jane Austen's taste wavered between the classical and the romantic, and nowhere is the conflict better illustrated than in her treatment of landscape. She liked gardens: she helped her mother care for them at

Steventon, Southampton and Chawton, and could name every flower in each. Her nicest heroines are all fond of flowers. There is a vicarage garden, Mr Collins's, in *Pride and Prejudice* and a greenhouse in *Sense and Sensibility*. But when it comes to larger houses, she belonged to the Brown rather than the Repton school: a garden had no place in the foreground of rolling parkland. She was, in other words, an opponent of the Picturesque.

The word often occurs in her writing, and it can bear different meanings. Originally it meant landscapes, natural or contrived, which looked like pictures by Claude and Poussin, extensions of the scene by planes through near, middle and far distances. Then came William Gilpin, of whose books Jane was a close student, who suggested that picturesqueness did not mean pretty pictures composed by Claude and, in his own way, by 'Capability' Brown, but their opposite, namely roughness and ruggedness, like craggy mountains, torrents, mouldering abbeys and tumbledown cottages smothered in ivy, previously thought 'horrid'. Uvedale Price, a foremost proponent of this version of the picturesque, went so far as to call a girl's squint beautiful because it was 'irregular', and praised the untamed landscape not because it was charming, but because it was awkward. The picturesque could therefore be found almost anywhere, in almost anything. A shaggy pony was picturesque, so was a ragged beggar, or a drowning man, or a Corsican bandit, or a wood in autumn, or a hamlet of thatched cottages like that which John Nash and Humphry Repton made in 1811 at Blaise, near Bristol. Even a classical building like the Parthenon was picturesque because it was a ruin.

Jane Austen embraced the first meaning of picturesqueness, orderliness and sublimity, but was doubtful about the second, irregularity for its own sake. When Elizabeth Bennet was asked by Darcy and two friends to join them, she replied that she would not: 'You are charmingly grouped ... The picturesque would be spoiled by admitting a fourth.' She is using the word as if it connoted propriety, balance. Gilpin would have said that it would only be picturesque if the triangularity of the group were broken, or if there must be three, let them stand apart at different distances and in clumsy attitudes. When irregularity occurs naturally, or in a building as the result of alteration or addition over a long period, Jane agrees that it can be beautiful, like Donwell Abbey in *Emma*,

> rambling and irregular, with many comfortable and one or two handsome rooms. It was just as it ought to be, and it looked what it was – and Emma felt an increasing respect for it, as the residence

The hamlet at Blaise, near Clifton, on which John Nash and Humphry Repton collaborated in 1811 as an exercise in the picturesque.

of a family of such true gentility, untainted in blood and understanding

as if good breeding shaped the house and the house encouraged good breeding. Where it is absent, an irregular house can be ungainly, like Winthrop in *Persuasion* which was 'without beauty and without dignity, an indifferent house, standing low and hemmed in by the barns and buildings of a farmyard.'

There are two entertaining passages in the novels where Jane Austen tries to face up to the problem of the Picturesque and decide whether she approves of it or not. The first occurs in *Sense and Sensibility* when Edward Ferrars is describing to Marianne Dashwood the pleasure he had had in walking through the Devon countryside, and she begins to question him on what had particularly delighted him:

'You must not inquire too far, Marianne – remember I have no knowledge of the picturesque, and I shall offend you by my ignorance and want of taste, if we come to particulars. I shall call hills steep, which ought to be bold. Surfaces strange and uncouth,

117

The countryside round Ibthorpe, north Hampshire, where Jane walked with her friends Mary and Martha Lloyd. The chalk downs clothed in trailing woods is the type of country that features prominently in the novels.

Opposite Woodside Farm, a resting place on one of Jane's favourite walks round the last of her homes, Chawton in Hampshire, where she wrote or rewrote all six of her published novels.

which ought to be irregular and rugged; and distant objects out of sight, which ought only to be indistinct through the soft medium of a hazy atmosphere . . . It exactly answers my idea of a fine country, because it unites beauty with utility – and I dare say it is a picturesque one too, because you admire it. I can easily believe it to be full of rocks and promontories, grey moss and brushwood, but those are all lost on me. I know nothing of the picturesque.'

She has caught the Gilpin/Price terminology precisely, but is not taken in by its sophisticated nonsense. Edward goes on:

'I like a fine prospect, but not on picturesque principles. I do not like crooked, twisted, blasted trees. I admire them much more if they are tall, straight and flourishing. I do not like ruined, tattered cottages. I am not fond of nettles, or thistles, or heath blossoms. I have more pleasure in a snug farmhouse than a watch-tower – and a troop of tidy happy villagers please me better than the finest banditti in the world.'

He is speaking for Jane Austen.

The second passage comes in *Northanger Abbey* when Henry Tilney, on a walk near Bath, lectures Catherine Morland on the picturesque, posing, unlike Edward Ferrars, as an authority and advocate:

He talked of foregrounds, distances and second distances – side-screens and perspectives – lights and shades: and Catherine was so hopeful a scholar that when they gained the top of Beechen Cliff, she voluntarily rejected the whole city of Bath as unworthy to make part of a landscape.

She was right. In either sense of the term, Bath seen clotted against its hillside, was definitely not picturesque.

The view over Bath from the summit of Beechen Cliff, as seen by Catherine Morland in *Northanger Abbey*. The beautiful Abbey lies in the centre and the successive crescents of eighteenth-century houses climb the hill behind.

VI

THE SEASIDE

The seascapes of southern England were so familiar to Jane Austen from her brothers' outward and homebound voyages that she could read them off as if she had a map in front of her, and the coast represented for her not just a succession of pleasant downs and bays, but an inviolable frontier guarded by the navy and militia for most of her adult life. It was behind this screen that the holiday-resorts developed. The coast was never declared, as it was in later wars, a prohibited area. The seaside holiday became fashionable at the very period when the Napoleonic threat was most acute. During their years in Bath the Austens were among the first families to make it an annual habit.

They had become familiar with the Kent coast, particularly Ramsgate and Deal, from visits while they stayed at Rowling and Godmersham, and Jane almost certainly knew Brighton, for in January 1799 she commiserated with Cassandra on being made to go there. But their regular seaside holidays did not begin till 1801 when they went to Sidmouth. In the following year it was Dawlish, and then Lyme Regis for two years running, 1803–4, at the height of the invasion scare, and probably Worthing in 1805, after which the death of George Austen and the impoverishment of the family put further trips beyond their means.

However, on moving to Southampton in 1806 they lived for another three years within a hundred yards of salt water, and their expeditions to Portsmouth put them in close touch with the sterner business of the sea – commerce and warfare. All this left a mark on the novels, even the earliest. In *Pride and Prejudice* we find the military stationed at Brighton where Wickham seduces Lydia Bennet, and the scenes in *Persuasion* at Lyme Regis and of *Mansfield Park* at Portsmouth are among the most famous she wrote. But it is above all in her unfinished *Sanditon* that Jane makes use of the seaside resort as a central location and examines the changes in building styles that the habit of holidaying by the sea had helped bring about.

Maggie Lane, has pointed out that the idea of seaside holidays had arisen from boredom with the sophisticated social life of spas like Bath and a new interest in Nature, which must include the sea at its wildest or most benign. 'In this sense', she wrote, 'Jane Austen stands exactly balanced between the eighteenth century way of thinking and the nineteenth', as she did in many other respects. In common with George III who frequented Weymouth and the Prince Regent who popularised Brighton, she believed the sea air to be beneficial to health, and she enjoyed sea-bathing, sometimes to excess, but with this difference from modern habit, that she preferred autumn, up to and including November, for these outings, and the early morning to the hottest part of the day for her dips.

George Austen first chose Sidmouth because his former pupil, Richard Buller, vicar of Colyton in east Devon, had invited him to bring his family on a visit to his beautiful church and capacious rectory. From there it was only a few miles to Sidmouth, a town on a curve of the coast between headlands of red sandstone. It was on a far smaller scale than Weymouth or Brighton, attracting only some three hundred visitors at the height of the season, but it had the obligatory Assembly Room, a stable where horses could be hired by the day, and some quite adventurous architecture, like the classicism of Fortfield Terrace begun in 1792 but never finished, and the speciality of Sidmouth, the *cottage ornée*, which was often quite a substantial house, decorated inside and out in playful arabesques. From the beach, which was narrowed to a thin strip by the tide, the shopping streets wormed inland.

Previous page Yachts and fishing boats clustered in the harbour at Lyme Regis.

Lyme Regis in Jane Austen's day was not the neatly tonsured resort one sees now, but a scattering of cottages on a tumbling shoreline, with a tiny harbour clutched from the sea by the famous curving pier known as the Cobb.

The present seafront at Lyme Regis seen from the Cobb. Even the prettier houses on the esplanade are later in date than Jane's visits to Lyme.

It was probably at Sidmouth that for the second time in her life (the first was with Tom Lefroy) she fell in love. It was not known to anyone but Cassandra, who revealed it in old age to Louisa Lefroy and Caroline Austen. Jane, she said, met a young clergyman who was on a visit to his brother, a local doctor, in a town where the Austens were holidaying. When they left, he asked to meet her again, a request that was readily granted, for to Cassandra he appeared a man 'whose charm of person, mind and manners was such that she thought him worthy to possess and likely to win her sister's love'. But at the moment when they expected him to return, they received a letter announcing his death. His name is unknown. This incident, which must have affected her profoundly, is sometimes held to be a reason why her Bath years were almost barren of writing. It seems unlikely. Like Charlotte Brontë's unrequited love for M. Heger, her Brussels professor, her loss would have been a motive for sublimating it on paper.

Dawlish was also a fairly new creation when the Austens went there in 1802. The white houses, now whiskered by television aerials, face the sea like guillemots on a cliff-ledge, awaiting action that seldom comes. It is twenty times the size of the 'bathing village' from which the resort began to emerge in the 1790s, but to this day it retains its shape and character better than the inflated dirigible of its neighbour Teignmouth, which the Austens may also have visited. Dawlish was a

The coast at Dawlish, Devon, which the Austens explored when on holiday there in 1802. The photograph shows a stretch of Brunel's South Devon Railway, the most exciting line in England, built in the 1840s.

curious destination for them, three days' journey by coach from Bath, and it had little to offer but a pretty situation, a poor library, some neat new buildings in which 'genteel lodgings' could be taken by the month, and some bathing machines on sands as ruddy as the surface of Mars. We know nothing about their visit, or where they stayed, but it must have made some impression on Jane, for in *Sense and Sensibility* she can make Robert Ferrars say, although facetiously, that 'it seemed rather surprising to him that anybody could live in Devonshire without living near Dawlish'.

The most memorable of their seaside resorts was Lyme Regis. They went there twice, and Jane wrote of it with unmistakable affection in *Persuasion*. She liked Lyme because it was unfashionable, contrasting it with Weymouth, which she called 'altogether a shocking place, without recommendation of any kind', although she had never been there. During the 1803 visit the two sisters and their parents probably stayed in a cottage called Wings overlooking the Cobb, where a garden is now named in her memory, and in the following year in a lodging house at the foot of the High Street, but neither of them can be positively identified, and John Fowles, the historian of Lyme and its most distinguished resident, says that they probably stayed both years in the extant Pyne House in Broad Street. She bathed almost daily, danced in the Assembly Room (demolished), walked on the Cobb, and with her brother Henry and his wife Eliza climbed the downland hills leading to Charmouth. She describes these walks in *Persuasion*, allowing herself, most unusually, the liberty of depicting an actual place with a degree of enthusiasm which shows how much it meant to her:

A very strange stranger it must be, who does not see charms in the immediate environs of Lyme, to make him wish to know it better. The scenes in its neighbourhood, Charmouth, with its high grounds and extensive sweeps of country, and still more, its sweet, retired bay, backed by dark cliffs, where fragments of low rock among the sands make it the happiest spot for watching the flow of the tide, for sitting in unwearied contemplation; the wooded varieties of the cheerful village of Up Lyme; and, above all, Pinny, with its green chasms between romantic rocks, where the scattered forest trees and orchards of luxuriant growth declare that many a generation must have passed away since the first partial falling of the cliff prepared the ground for such a state, where a scene so wonderful and so lovely is exhibited, as may more than equal any of the resembling scenes of the far-famed Isle of Wight: these places must be visited, and visited again to make the worth of Lyme understood.

The sentiment, if not the phrasing and the grammar, does her credit.

The town itself made little appeal to her. 'There is nothing to admire in the buildings' is her verdict in *Persuasion*, but wrongly, for the line of small houses, water-mills and gardens, reaching up the stream from the shore, is still as pleasant as when Miss Mitford played there as a child, in the garden of a house where the Earl of Chatham once lived. Jane would not have been impressed by this information, any more than she was by memories of the Duke of Monmouth who landed at Lyme in 1685 at the outset of his disastrous expedition. Instead, she praises the bay, animated by holiday-makers and furnished by their bathing machines, and particularly the Cobb, the sea-wall which curves round like a hand held out to salvage struggling ships and protect the tiny harbour from wind and shingle. It is a considerable work of engineering if not of architecture, forming walks on two levels, from the uppermost of which Louisa Musgrove fell when jumping down into Captain Wentworth's arms by the steps knows as Granny's Teeth, the single piece of masonry in Jane Austen's fiction which can be identified for certain. The bay itself is not as she saw it, except for the splendid view eastwards along the coast to Portland. It was not protected by a

Lyme Regis, the view from Timber Hill.

Below The Cobb at Lyme Regis is a gigantic breakwater first constructed in the middle ages when it was regarded as one of the architectural wonders of England, but it was not fully clad with the present Portland stone until the time of Jane Austen's visit to Lyme. From the upper level descend the stone steps, known as Granny's teeth (*right*), from which the flirtatious Louisa Musgrove threw herself into the arms of Captain Wentworth in *Persuasion*, and missing, collapsed at his feet in a faint.

continuous sea-wall till the 1850s, and the mixture of Regency-type villas and ice-cream parlours which now form its backdrop is a poor substitute for the sloping cliff and scattered cottages of her day.

Sanditon describes a seaside town in the making, 'a young and rising bathing-place', according to Mr Parker, its developer, based upon a quiet village with a manor house attached. Mr Parker's smaller house, two miles from the sea, lay in a sheltered fold of the downs, without air or view, and he had abandoned it to a tenant, building for himself Trafalgar House ('I almost wish I had not named it Trafalgar – for Waterloo is more the thing now') which greeted the astonished traveller as he surmounted the highest point, a 'light, elegant building' with a veranda and French and Venetian windows, all in the newest and most perfect taste. Nearby is a *cottage ornée*, like Sidmouth's, a charming retreat, comfortable inside, picturesque outside; and nearer to Trafalgar were a library and a hotel, neither of which was as well stocked with books or guests as Mr Parker would wish. But give him time. As the place develops, so will its trade.

The new Sanditon is not wholly absurd. Jane's heroine, Charlotte, finds 'amusement enough in standing at her ample Venetian window, and looking over the miscellaneous foreground of unfinished building, waving linen, and tops of houses, to the sea, dancing and sparkling in sunshine and freshness'. Jane recognises that change must come, and does not despair of men like Mr Parker who is straightforward, well disposed, anxious to succeed in his enterprise and make an honest fortune. He is introducing novelty without vulgarity. His new houses are not shoddy or ill-planned. They are works of architecture, a new element in the land and seascape, and Jane was not going to turn up her nose too haughtily. In this last fragment of her writing, composed when she was mortally ill, she was still experimenting with something new in style and subject. She was contemplating a future that she would never know, and exploring once more the conflict that had always interested her, between the old manner and the new, represented here by the ancient house in its hidden valley of the Downs and the gleaming new Sanditon which boldly faces the noontime sun across a Channel finally, in 1817, swept clear of England's enemy.

When the Austens moved to Southampton in 1806 they lived in a corner of Castle Square, an area of the city so extensively rebuilt that the site of their house cannot now be precisely identified. The garden, it was said, led to the medieval ramparts, which at that time were lapped by the tidal sea, and there would have been a view across the Solent to the wooded horizon of the New Forest. In the 1850s the

The High Street, Southampton, in 1808, by Tobias Young. It was then (when the Austens knew it) less a port than a spa. Its graceful streets were ruined by Victorian development and the bombing of the Second World War.

foreshore was reclaimed and developed for fast traffic and industrial dockside buildings, and the peace of the Austens' garden and the slow passing of sailing ships is now unrecoverable. Moreover, little of the ancient architecture of this once beautiful city remains. The Bargate, one of the finest medieval gateways in Britain, and the Westgate, a sallyport where Henry V embarked for Agincourt and the Pilgrims for New England, are isolated reminders of the past. From the eighteenth century we still have the Dolphin Hotel with its two-breasted façade which contains the Long Room in which Jane Austen had danced as a child when she was at school there, and now again, in her early thirties.

Her family were happy there. The house in Castle Square was commodious and old-fashioned and they shared it with Jane's brother Francis and his newly married wife, Mary Gibson. Martha Lloyd (who was to become Francis's second wife) came to live with them after her mother's death. Southampton was not only a busy port. It was also a spa. The combination of the two made it a favourite place for Miss Mitford who wrote to a friend in 1812, 'Have you ever been at that lovely spot which combines all that is buxom, blythe and debonair in society – that charming town which is not a watering place only because

131

Left The Austens' house at Southampton stood a little way inland from this stretch of the medieval walls, and its garden probably led to the ramparts which at that period directly overlooked the sea. The ferry connected the town with Portsmouth.

Below The Dolphin Hotel on the High Street is one of the few surviving buildings in Southampton which Jane Austen is known to have frequented. She danced there as a child, and again when the Austens returned in 1806. Pevsner calls it the best eighteenth-century building in the city.

it is something better?' And she spoke of 'the total absence of the vulgar hurry of business or the chilling apathy of fashion' – negative qualities that would have appealed to Jane Austen. Southampton was provincial, unselfconscious. Frank soon left them, to command a warship sent on convoy to China, so the household was reduced to five women – Jane, Cassandra, Mrs Austen, Mary and Martha Lloyd – to which a sixth was added in 1807, Mary Jane, Frank's daughter born in his absence.

It is surprising that Jane wrote nothing during her two-and-a-half years in Southampton when the will and the capacity to write trembled so close beneath the surface that books bubbled from her as soon as she left. She had little more to occupy her time than she had had in Bath. Southampton figures but once in her writings, in *Love and Friendship*, which she wrote as a child, and then it is associated with 'stinking fish', but Portsmouth provided an important scene in *Mansfield Park*, when Fanny Price revisits her parents after an absence of a dozen years to find her mother harassed by childcare and her father uncouth and alcoholic.

Portsmouth in the year after Trafalgar was in a sense the heart of the nation. A main reason why the Austens chose to live in Southampton was its proximity to the naval base to which at any moment Francis or Charles might return or be summoned. Mr and Mrs Austen boarded HMS *Neptune* in 1802 to see the conditions below decks of a man-of-war, and although there is no record that Jane ever went there, the accuracy of her description of it in her novel, and the ease with which it could be approached by water from Southampton, makes it almost certain that she did. It was a seamen's town in contrast to genteel Southampton, burly and bawdy, but the dockyard buildings, completed in 1788, were large, practical and graceful, symbols of the pride Englishmen took in their Navy. The great ships would beat their way through the narrow entrance to the harbour, unfurl their sails and spill their brutalised crews into the taverns and brothels of the Point, a scene immortalised by Rowlandson in his least sentimental manner.

Mansfield Park catches something of the contrast between the harshness of naval life and its nobility. The Prices lived in 'a narrow street leading from the High Street', and Fanny entered the house through a mean corridor off which opened a parlour 'so small that her first conviction was of its being only a passage-room to something better'. Upstairs there were bedrooms which resounded to the yelling of the smaller children. Fanny was appalled. 'The smallness of the house and thinness of the walls brought everything so close to her that, added to the fatigue of her journey, and all her recent agitation, she hardly knew how to bear it.' The behaviour of her parents, their apparent

133

Left The entrance to
Portsmouth Harbour from
the end of the ramparts where
Fanny Price walked during
her visit to her parents from
Mansfield Park.

Below Lombard Street,
Portsmouth, the elegance of
which reminds one that even
junior naval officers were
housed elegantly if not
comfortably. It was just such
a street that Jane describes in
Mansfield Park as the squalid
home of the Price family.

indifference to their long-separated daughter, the slovenliness of the servant, added to her distress. Clearly Jane Austen is relating the meanness of the house to the meanness of Fanny's treatment, one being the prime cause of the other. 'In her uncle's house [Mansfield Park] there would have been a consideration of times and seasons, a regulation of subject, a propriety, an attention towards everybody which there was not here.' There speaks Jane in Fanny's guise, not from snobbishness but from the habit of decorum which, once instilled, would not be stifled even by dire poverty or the humblest home.

'A narrow street leading from the High Street', might be Lombard Street, one of the few eighteenth-century streets in central Portsmouth to be spared the bombing of the last war. The appearance of this row of small houses, so neat, so attractive, is not inconsistent with interiors as ramshackle and ill-kempt as the Prices'. Jane was so accustomed to good design in building that she would not have given Lombard Street a second look, except perhaps to glance through a downstairs window as she passed and notice that it was an unhygienic human warren. Like Fanny, she would derive solace from walking the ramparts:

> The day was uncommonly lovely. It was really March; but it was April in its mild air, brisk soft wind and bright sun, occasionally clouded for a minute; and everything looked so beautiful under the influence of such a sky; the effects of the shadows pursuing each other on the ships at Spithead and the island beyond, with the ever-varying hues of the sea, now at high water, dancing in its glee and dashing against the ramparts with so fine a sound, produced altogether such a combination of charms for Fanny, as made her gradually almost careless of the circumstances under which she felt them.

Fanny's enjoyment of that walk can only derive from Jane's experience on that very spot. Such was the use she made of treasured moments from the Southampton years. The sea enticed her. She lingered by its shores like her characters in *Persuasion*, 'as all must linger and gaze on a first return to the sea, who ever deserved to look at it at all.'

VII

EXCURSIONS TO CASTLES, ABBEYS AND CHURCHES

When Jane Austen was barely sixteen, she sat down at Steventon to write *The History of England: by a partial, prejudiced and ignorant Historian. N.B. There will be very few dates in this History*, and she kept her word, both as regards dates and prejudice. The History is lopped at each end: it starts with Henry IV and ends with Charles I. Its main purpose, the inquisitorial authoress confessed, was to prove the innocence of Mary Queen of Scots 'and to abuse Elizabeth', but she clouts nearly every other monarch too, like Henry VIII: 'The Crimes and Cruelties of this Prince were too numerous to be mentioned, and nothing can be said in his vindication, but that his abolishing Religious Houses and leaving them to the ruinous depredations of Time has been of infinite use to the Landscape of England.'

Her mischievous attitude to the past persisted throughout her life, but there is no further proof that she thought ruined abbeys and castles an adornment to the countryside. To her the Middle Ages were like fields of corn reduced to stubble, uninteresting, and beyond them she did not even bother to enquire. If Box Hill was once an Iron Age camp, what of it? It was an agreeable place for a picnic. Nonetheless, she could hardly avoid the evidence of time. It was all around her, not so much in the neighbourhood of Steventon which was archaeologically barren, but in places like Reading where she and Cassandra had attended a school in the gatehouse of a twelfth-century abbey run by Mrs Latournelle who, more interestingly, had an artificial leg made of cork; or at Oxford where the old buildings were at least habitable, but they made so little impression on Jane that she wrote, aged thirteen, 'I never but once was at Oxford in my life, and I am sure I never wish to go there again. They dragged me through so many dismal chapels, dusty libraries and greasy halls that it gave me the vapours for two days afterwards'. This from the daughter of a Fellow of St John's College and great-niece of a Master of Balliol.

Only two medieval castles figure in her life or books, and she saw both of them within a few days of each other when on a visit to

Stoneleigh in 1806. One was the amazing ruin of Kenilworth Castle, which rises from green fields in jagged red stalagmites: the other, Warwick Castle, still intact with its romantic crenellations. Both sights were included in the Gardiners' northern journey in *Pride and Prejudice*, but neither is closely described.

She reserved her comments on all castles for a fake. It is one of her most elaborate jokes, if joke it was, for if it was not, she was for once untrue to her habit of meticulous accuracy. The incident occurs in *Northanger Abbey*. John Thorpe is proposing to Catherine Morland an expedition to Blaise Castle, near Clifton:

'Blaise Castle!', cried Catherine. 'What is that?'
'The finest place in England – worth going fifty miles at any time to see.'
'What, is it really a castle, an old castle?'
'The oldest in the kingdom.'
'But is it like what one reads of?'
'Exactly – the very same.'
'But now really – are there towers and long galleries?'
'By dozens.'

The 'castle' was not the oldest in the kingdom: it had been built as a folly only thirty years before, in 1766, by Thomas Farr, a Bristol merchant. There are three towers, castellated and pierced by arrow-slits, but no long galleries, for there was no room inside for more than a large circular drawing-room and a kitchen beneath it. Catherine did not after all join the expedition, but it is worth speculating whether Thorpe would have sustained his joke in the hope that Catherine would be too innocent to suspect it or too ignorant to detect it. Jane could have been to Blaise during an early visit to Bath when she was drafting *Northanger Abbey*, and it is just possible that she was taken in by its spurious look of antiquity; but a more likely explanation is that she knew exactly what Thorpe was doing in teasing Catherine into accompanying him, and assumed that the reader would know too. It is an ingenious piece of comedy at the expense of antiquaries and romantic novelists like Mrs Radcliffe.

We know of one other expedition she made to a medieval ruin, and this time the ruin was genuine and she had no mocking intentions. It was to entertain her niece and nephew, Fanny and William Knight, aged fourteen and nine. In September 1807 they went by boat to Netley Abbey on the shores of Southampton Water. It was a large party, consisting in Jane, Cassandra, Edward and his wife Elizabeth, Henry

Previous page Kenilworth Castle, Warwickshire, which Jane visited in 1806, as did the Gardiners in *Pride and Prejudice*. Still standing is the huge Norman keep with walls twenty feet thick. It is one of the grandest ruins in England.

Opposite above Warwick Castle, today one of the most visited castles in England, standing on a steep cliff above the River Avon. This too was on the Austen itinerary in 1806.

Opposite below Blaise Castle, near Bristol, a folly built in 1766 by a merchant who had made a fortune in sugar and became Mayor of the city. In *Northanger Abbey* Jane made use of it to tease the innocent Catherine Morland and poke fun at the antiquarianism which was then the indulgence of the country gentry.

The ruins of Netley Abbey, a Cistercian foundation which after the Reformation was temporarily transformed into a splendid house. It stood on the shores of Southampton Water, and Jane Austen, with a niece and nephew, made an expedition there by boat in 1807. Her niece, Fanny Knight, was more impressed by it than Jane.

Austen, and the two children. We do not have Jane's account of the Abbey, but we do have Fanny's, in a letter to her old governess, Miss Chapman, recently discovered by Deirdre Le Faye in the Kent County Archives:

> Never was there anything in the known world to be compared to that compound of everything that is striking, ancient and majestic: we were struck dumb with admiration, and I wish I could write anything that would come near to the sublimity of it, but that is utterly impossible as nothing I could say would give you a distant idea of its extreme beauty . . .

and so on, which for a fourteen-year-old is not a bad attempt at contemporary astonishment-writing. In 1807 Netley Abbey was over-

140

grown with ivy, and trees sprouted from its courtyards. Its remains would scarcely be standing today if English Heritage had not stripped it clean and stabilised the masonry. Although it was one of the poorest Cistercian abbeys, it made a fine house after the Dissolution; the nave of the church was turned into a vast banqueting hall. But this too was abandoned, and the medieval buildings reasserted themselves over the Elizabethan. Jane would not have joined in her niece's rhapsodies. She would have thought the Abbey curious, more mutilated than sublime, and would have most regretted the loss of the house which was temporarily contained within it.

Her final revision of *Northanger Abbey* was completed in 1803, four years before the expedition to Netley and three years before her visit to Stoneleigh Abbey with which Northanger is most often compared. Her motives seem to have been not only to use the book as a vehicle for ridiculing the Gothic novel, but to examine in detail how monastic buildings could be transformed into a house. When she arrived at Stoneleigh in 1806 with her mother and her mother's first cousin, the Rev. Thomas Leigh, who had unexpectedly inherited it, she might have exclaimed, 'But this is Northanger Abbey!'

The similarity is indeed remarkable. It had been a Cistercian Abbey like Netley, founded in 1154. At the Dissolution it had eventually come to the Leigh family as 'a heap of ruins', apart from its beautiful gatehouse which still stands intact at a short distance from the house. An Elizabethan mansion was built on the monastic foundations, turning the Cloister into an internal courtyard. When Edward, the 3rd Lord Leigh, married an heiress in 1714, he had the west wing rebuilt by a local architect, Francis Smith, on a monumental scale. It is a great encrusted cliff of stone, beautifully executed in the Chatsworth tradition. Inside, the main rooms are richly furnished and decorated with some of the best plasterwork to survive from the eighteenth century. The Saloon with its scagliola columns is one of the finest of its date in England, wonderfully light and distinguished, and the medallions on its walls modelled in low relief, are still as sharp as newly minted coins. The rooms along this floor are arranged *en suite*, creating a sense of expectation and surprise, the expectation that there is a lot more to find, and the surprise of finding it.

Mrs Austen described their astonishment in a letter to her daughter-in-law:

Everything is very grand and very fine and very large. The house is larger than I could have supposed. We can *now* find our way about it, I mean the best part; as to the offices (which were the old Abbey),

Stoneleigh Abbey, near Coventry, was inherited by an Austen cousin in 1806 shortly before Mrs Austen, Jane and Cassandra visited him at his Adlestrop parsonage. They went with him to view his amazing property, an Elizabethan house of which part remained *left*, and a monumental entrance front *below* which had been built in 1714. Mrs Austen, staggered by its size, counted, correctly, forty-five windows.

Opposite The Saloon at Stoneleigh in the 1714 wing contains elaborate plasterwork, among the most beautiful in England, and scagliola columns. It has been suggested that the stuccoist was an Italian, Francesco Vassali.

142

Mr Leigh almost despairs of ever finding his way about them. There are forty-five windows in front (which is quite straight with a flat roof), fifteen in a row. You go up considerable flights of steps (some offices are under the house) into a large hall; on the right hand the dining parlour, within that the breakfast room, where we generally sit, and reason good 'tis the only room (except the chapel) that looks towards the river [Avon]. On the left hand of the hall is the best drawing-room; within that a smaller; these rooms are rather gloomy brown wainscot and dark crimson furniture, so we never use them but to walk through them to the old picture gallery. Behind the smaller drawing-room is the state bedchamber, with a high dark crimson velvet bed: an *alarming* apartment just fit for a heroine: the old gallery opens into it; behind the hall and parlours is a passage all across the house containing three staircases and two small back parlours.

And so she prattles on. She might have been General Tilney conducting Catherine Morland round Northanger Abbey.

The rooms are today much as she describes them, except that the breakfast room, now renamed 'Jane Austen's Room', contains a vast bed used by Queen Victoria on her visit in 1858. Jane drew one feature from Stoneleigh, the balconied chapel at Sotherton in *Mansfield Park*, but otherwise the mansions of her later novels borrow details from houses she already knew.

From where, then, came the idea for Northanger Abbey? No house remotely resembling it was known to her in Kent or Hampshire, but from her reading and her study of illustrated books and print rooms like that at The Vyne, she would have known that such houses existed, converted from abbeys at the Reformation because they were well built and usually sited in agreeable meadows beside a stream. As they drove to Northanger, Henry Tilney aroused in Catherine (who was tingling with excitement) the prospect of a house which might have figured in Ann Radcliffe's Gothic novel *The Mysteries of Udolpho* which she had been reading with mixed terror and delight. She was led to expect a great stone building like Bodiam Castle in Sussex: frightful cavernous halls, and gloomy passages ending in a door which would admit her by the light of a guttering candle to a vast bedroom which the housekeeper told her, before leaving for the night, was undoubtedly haunted.

In fact Northanger Abbey was nothing of the kind. Its exterior was welcoming, its rooms light and handsome. There were many of them, and slowly as Catherine's tour progresses, we can make out the plan of the house. As at Stoneleigh, there was a central courtyard which was

Right The chapel at Stoneleigh from its gallery, which is entered from the higher level. This bears so close a resemblance to the chapel at Sotherton described in *Mansfield Park* ('its profusion of mahogany and the crimson velvet cushions appearing over the ledge of the family gallery') that, for once, one can hazard the guess that Jane Austen drew it from life.

Below The internal courtyard at Stoneleigh, once the cloister of the medieval Abbey, was remodelled to form the sixteenth-century house. All this part of Stoneleigh has striking affinities with Northanger Abbey, but Jane Austen had revised her novel three years before her visit.

once the Cloister, and round three sides of it were ranged a lofty hall, a large drawing-room, a small drawing-room, a breakfast room, a library, a billiards room, a gun room, and upstairs, two long galleries and innumerable bedrooms. To Catherine's disappointment, all Gothic vestiges had been discarded for 'the profusion and elegance of modern taste': there was not even a cobweb. Her bedroom was not in the least alarming. She found the place spooky only because of General Tilney's strange character. In conformity with her previous conception of the house, she imagined him his wife's murderer, when he was nothing more than a snob and a domestic tyrant. He was also a manic improver. Every detail of the house, garden and estate was governed by his whim and fancy. His father had torn down the fourth side of the quadrangle to replace it by a service wing, and the General had equipped it with every modern device to ease the labour of the servants of whom there were so many that Catherine thought she never saw the same one twice. But the General's tour is still not complete:

> They returned to the hall that the chief staircase might be ascended, and the beauty of its wood and ornaments of rich carving might be

The gatehouse was built by the sixteenth Abbot of Stoneleigh in 1346, and is the only substantial structure of the medieval abbey to survive.

146

Jane Austen, the daughter of a vicar, worshipped in many churches like this one at Hurstbourne Tarrant, where her brother James married Mary Lloyd.

pointed out [like Godinton's?]: having gained the top, they turned in the opposite direction from the gallery in which her room lay, and shortly entered one on the same plan, but superior in length and breadth. She was here shown successively into three large bed-chambers, with their dressing-rooms, most completely and handsomely fitted up: everything that money and taste could do, to give comfort and elegance to apartments, had been bestowed on these.

Nowhere does Jane Austen give a more minute description of a house, and she does it twice, once as Catherine Morland might imagine it, fed by Henry Tilney's lugubrious fantasies, and once as it really is. Evidently the reader is supposed to admire the Abbey, but not wish to live in it. It was not to Jane's taste. It was too grand, too expensive, too perfect, and it was organised with the sort of brutal efficiency that characterised its owner.

Then there were the churches. Considering that she was a parson's daughter, and that religion and ordination play a large part in her novels, it is remarkable that not a single church is described, and that nobody seems to enter one except to be married. Emma Woodhouse skips church even on Christmas Day with the flimsiest of excuses. It appears that in her youth Jane was conventionally devout, prepared to ridicule the more absurd clergymen like Mr Collins (so does Charlotte Brontë, another parson's daughter, in *Shirley*), but her artistry was such that in mocking the Church she confirmed its eternal verities. In later life, her faith was profound. She could compose prayers of this kind: 'Teach us to understand the sinfulness of our hearts ... Incline us oh God! to think humbly of ourselves, to be severe only in the examination of our own conduct, to consider our fellow-creatures with kindness.' Such piety cannot be simulated. Yet she could accept that young men of good family could enter the Church without training or dedication, and almost without belief. Edmund Bertram, in *Mansfield Park*, whose faith was unquestioned, was exceptional. There was a trade in 'livings' which was almost cynical. Few of her patrons felt much shame in absenteeism or in the snobbish dependence of the rectory on the great house. Robert Ferrars in *Sense and Sensibility* speaks of his brother's forthcoming ordination in the cruellest terms:

> The idea of Edward's being a clergyman and living in a small parsonage house, diverted him beyond measure; and when to that was added the fanciful imagery of Edward reading prayers in a white surplice, and publishing the banns of marriage between John Smith and Mary Brown, he could conceive nothing more ridiculous.

Yet his ordination went ahead, and Jane saw little wrong with it. She was not attacking the clergy: she was observing it. She did not find shocking the habits of her age.

Her links with the church were prolific. Her father, two of her brothers, her maternal grandfather, and several uncles, cousins and friends were all clergymen. Cassandra was engaged to one: Jane herself fell in love with another. The result was a chain of rectories and vicarages across the country at which the Austens could be sure of a welcome, and many of these houses were interesting enough to play quite a part in Jane's architectural education, but rarely the churches, which were much more beautiful and historic. Many of them survive almost unchanged by restoration.

The most familiar to her was, of course, her father's church at Steventon, St Nicholas's, which was essentially thirteenth-century, very plain inside and out, visually the dullest, except to an archaeologist, of the whole series. Godmersham's was handsomer, but here there have been major changes, by Butterfield in 1865, who removed the family box-pews in which Jane sat Sunday after Sunday, replaced them by the south aisle, and capped the tower by a pyramid roof. The loveliest were the churches of Hurstbourne Tarrant, where James Austen married Mary Lloyd; Colyton with its octagonal lantern imposed in the fifteenth century on the square Norman tower; and Great Bookham, Emma's 'Highbury'. Jane may also have visited Upton Pyne in Devon during her family's holiday at Dawlish in 1802, for in *Sense and Sensibility* she places 'Barton' four miles north of Exeter, like Upton, and this lovely fourteenth-century church could have been in her mind when she wrote of the wedding of Elinor Dashwood and Edward Ferrars.

But the rectories remained uppermost in her mind. Several have long since vanished – Steventon, Deane, Great Bookham, Kintbury – but their appearance is in most cases known from prints and drawings. Kintbury, for instance, near Newbury in Berkshire, was the home of Rev. Thomas Fowle and his wife Jane, a sister of Mrs Lloyd of Ibthorpe. They had four clever sons, two of whom, Fulwar and Tom, had been George Austen's pupils and close friends of James. Fulwar married Eliza Lloyd, and Tom became engaged to Cassandra Austen, but he died of yellow fever in the West Indies before he could marry her. Kintbury was therefore tinged with melancholy for all the Austens, but Jane loved it, returning there for the last time in the spring of 1816, a year before she died. The Rectory was pulled down by a rich vicar in about 1860 (only a rough painting of it survives in the church hall)

The Rectory at Kintbury, Berkshire, since demolished, of which this is the only known picture. Jane Austen was a frequent guest there. The vicar, Thomas Fowle, married a sister of Mrs Lloyd of Ibthorpe, and Cassandra Austen was briefly engaged to their son Tom, who died of yellow fever before they could be married.

Above Godmersham church, the Norman church of Jane's brother Edward Austen (Knight), which is the church most closely associated with her.

Opposite above The Rectory of Hamstall Ridware in Staffordshire, the furthest north that Jane Austen ever travelled, where she and her mother stayed in 1806 with another vicar-cousin. It is a beautiful Georgian house of 1724, little altered since then, proof that vicars of that date may have been as poor as church-mice but were handsomely housed.

Opposite below Many vicars were among the Austens' relatives, and Jane travelled the country as a guest in their vicarages. Adlestrop Rectory in Gloucestershire was one of the most elegant, the home of her mother's cousin, Thomas Leigh, where they stayed in 1806 during the Midland tour.

and a new, larger rectory was built on its site beside the Kennet and Avon Canal.

The Rector of Adlestrop was Thomas Leigh, Mrs Austen's first cousin, and she and her daughters were staying there in 1806 when he heard to his astonishment that he had inherited Stoneleigh Abbey. He was reluctant to leave his vicarage for so enormous a house, and it is indeed delightful, facing an idealised Cotswold landscape towards Stow-on-the-Wold. It was probably built about 1670, but 'improved'. Four rooms *en suite* open out to each other on a sunny ground floor. One is reminded there of Catherine Morland's wish: 'There was nothing so charming to her imagination as the unpretending comfort of a well-connected parsonage.'

From Stoneleigh, where the three Austens went from Adlestrop, they continued to Staffordshire, the furthest north that Jane Austen ever travelled if one discounts a popular theory that she based Pemberley on a visit to Chatsworth in Derbyshire when she was very young. They stayed for five weeks with Edward Cooper, another of Mrs Austen's

Court Lodge, formerly the Rectory of Wrotham, near Sevenoaks, Kent, was designed by Samuel Wyatt. Jane spent two nights there, in 1813, and it was probably the only Regency house she knew well from the inside. Houses of this type figure in her last (unfinished) novel, *Sanditon*.

cousins, the vicar of Hamstall Ridware, a village eight miles north of Lichfield. The Rectory is an excellent red-brick house of 1724 built for the vicar, and the only external alteration since that date has been Edward's modest extensions at the back. The notion that Delaford in *Sense and Sensibility* is based upon it must be fallacious, because Colonel Brandon's house was much larger and Jane Austen did not visit Hamstall till ten years after she had written the novel. But the neat triangular relationship between church, manor house and rectory is perfectly exemplified here, and is one of Jane's favourite fictional devices.

Finally there is Wrotham in Kent. Jane spent two nights in its Rectory in November 1813 as the guest of its vicar George Moore, on her way from Godmersham to London, and her brother Edward was with her. The connection was through Harriot Moore, the vicar's wife and Edward's sister-in-law. The vicar, son of an Archbishop of Canterbury, was wealthy enough, and audacious enough, to demolish the old vicarage at Wrotham and in 1801 commission Samuel Wyatt to design a new one (now Court Lodge) in the nicest, cleanest, fanciest, whitest, freshest Regency style. There is an entrance porch balanced on four Greek columns, and on the garden side a 'segmental bow' topped by a shallow lead dome. It was perhaps the only Regency house that Jane Austen ever stayed in, and she may have thought of it when writing *Sanditon*. The visit, however, was not without mishaps:

Owing to a difference of clocks, [she wrote to Cassandra on reaching London] the coachman did not bring the carriage so soon as he ought by half-an-hour; anything like a breach of punctuality was a great offence, and Mr Moore was very angry, which I was rather glad of. I wanted to see him angry, and though he spoke to his servant in a very loud voice and with a good deal of heat, I was happy to perceive that he did not scold Harriot at all.

VIII

JANE'S TRIUMPH AT CHAWTON

The Austens – now only Mrs Austen, Jane and Cassandra, with Martha Lloyd – moved to Chawton in July 1809, and it was to be Jane's home for the last years of her life. They had considered settling in Wye, near Godmersham, then at Alton, Chawton's market-town, but they finally decided to accept an offer from Edward Austen to refurbish for them his bailiff's cottage at Chawton, within a few minutes walk of Chawton House, which, together with Godmersham and the living of Steventon, he had inherited from the Knights, whose surname he was to adopt in 1812.

It was a small house rather than a cottage, lying at the busy junction of the roads to Winchester and Portsmouth. Architecturally it was a mess, remedied by its decent seventeenth-century brickwork and a garden on two sides. It lacks Georgian symmetry and proportion because until recently it has been much abused. It was an inn before it became the bailiff's house, and on the death of Jane's sister in 1845, it was divided into three lodgings for labourers. The Jane Austen Memorial Trust, to whom Edward Carpenter gave the house in 1948, have restored it as near as possible to its appearance in her day and furnished it appropriately, often with possessions that she knew, but in some respects it remains a puzzle.

We know that Edward blocked a ground-floor window that faced the road and replaced it by another on the garden side, but this would hardly have cost the eighty pounds he spent on the house in 1809, and one must ask whether he did not also add the two bedrooms at the back which are not now shown to visitors. Jane, before she had been there and before the improvements were begun, mentioned six, and one can count six, some very small, in the main part of the house. If they had in fact eight, it would not have been too many for four members of the family, two servants, and as many as four guests at a time.

A more fundamental structural problem concerns the entrance. The front door now opens from the road into the dining-parlour, a most improbable arrangement, perhaps resorted to when the house was

divided into three. Between the parlour and the drawing-room, is a narrow corridor called the Vestibule. It seems likely that in the Austens' day the street-door opened into it (Caroline Austen's 'good-sized entrance'), in the manner of other old houses in the vicinity, and that stairs would have risen from the far end. The famous 'creaking door', which according to Caroline warned Jane of visitors in time to hide her manuscripts, cannot have been in the dining-room where she wrote, since an intruder would have been inside the room simultaneously with the creak, and is more likely to have opened off the Vestibule into the garden or kitchen.

Caroline, who knew the house well as a child, called it 'altogether a comfortable ladylike establishment', well furnished and well kept. Spruce it must always have been, for that was the habit of the family, but too small to be comfortable and too simple to be ladylike. Jane and Cassandra shared a bedroom, and there was no 'dressing-room' as there had been at Steventon, in fact no privacy for either of them. Passersby could look into the dining-room window as the Austens sat at breakfast, and when it was cleared away, Jane would write at the minute pedestal table that is still exhibited there. If she played the piano, she would do so in the early morning, 'so that she might

Chawton Cottage, near Alton, Hampshire, where the three Austen women went to live in 1809. The garden front *previous page* and from the Winchester road *above*.

156

not disturb the family' (Caroline again), but the house would have resounded to her playing, specially if she accompanied it, as she often did, by singing the popular airs of the day.

The garden was larger than it is now. There was a shrubbery big enough for walking in, a vegetable garden, and a field for two donkeys. They also kept chickens. The flower garden was a main source of occupation and pleasure to them. In May 1811 Jane wrote to her sister, who was at Godmersham:

> The chickens are all alive and fit for the table, but we save them for something grand. Some of the flower seeds are coming up very well, but your mignonette makes a wretched appearance ... Our young piony at the foot of the fir tree has just blown and looks very handsome, and the whole of the shrubbery border will soon be very gay with pinks and sweet-williams, in addition to the columbines in full bloom. The syringas, too, are coming out. We are likely to get a good crop of Orleans plums ...

and so on. It indicates a great appreciation of the fruits of other people's labours. Mrs Austen was the gardener in the family. But we know that Jane did plant an oak sapling from Chawton House. When a change in the garden's boundary in 1985 put the full-grown tree into the care of the roads department of Hampshire County Council, they promptly chopped it down.

Alton was a pretty town. The welcoming sinuosity of its High Street, the attractive Georgian houses which still flank parts of it, the Assembly Hall, the bank, the church and the many inns (for it was an important posting town) made it an ideal centre for news, shopping and entertainment. It was only a mile from Chawton, and Jane would often walk there by the lanes and fields, calling at the lovely Wyards Farm *en route*, a house dated 1691 in dark bricks across its façade, where her favourite niece Anna came to live in 1815 with her husband Ben Lefroy. Jane was still a great walker, and the countryside was richer than Steventon's, 'a very abrupt uneven country, full of hills and woods, and therefore full of birds', as Gilbert White wrote of his own parish of Selborne, only a mile or two away. The whole Chawton estate was open to her, great oak and beech woods alternating with chalky meadows and felicitous farms like Upper Woodside.

The Austens made no friends at Chawton comparable to those they had known round Steventon. They had no carriage other than a donkey-cart (which is still to be seen in an outhouse behind the cottage), so 'their visits did not extend far', wrote Caroline. 'There were a few

families living in the village, but no great intimacy was kept up with any of them – they were upon friendly but rather distant terms with all.' Chawton House was the only nearby mansion, and their next-door neighbour, William Prowting, Deputy Lieutenant for Hampshire, had two unmarried daughters who were on calling terms at the cottage, little more. There was also Miss Benn, the impoverished sister of the Rector of Farringdon, who rented a decrepit cottage in Chawton, and John Papillon, its bachelor vicar, whom Jane first heard of in 1808 through Mrs Knight, who tactfully suggested that Jane might marry him. 'I am very much obliged to Mrs Knight', she answered through Cassandra, 'for such a proof of the interest she takes in me – and she may depend upon it, that I *will* marry Mr Papillon, whatever may be his reluctance or my own – I owe her much more than such a trifling sacrifice.'

Wyards Farm, near Alton, the lovely seventeenth-century house where Anna Austen (Lefroy) lived after her marriage in much greater comfort than her aunts and Mrs Austen at Chawton Cottage a mile away.

There was no need for local intimacies because they had each other. Martha Lloyd, terribly pockmarked by smallpox when young, was full of cheerfulness and household help, and in two of the last letters that Jane ever wrote, she mentions Martha with tender affection as one who cared for her in her illness. She was regarded almost as one of the family, which she became absolutely ten years after Jane's death, by marrying the man she had always loved, Francis Austen, Jane's sailor brother, when she was a spinster of sixty-three and he a widower of fifty-four.

The brothers were frequent visitors to Chawton. Henry came down from London (there was a branch of his bank at Alton), James from Steventon where he was still Rector, Edward from Godmersham, Francis and Charles when on leave from their ships, with their growing tribe of children, and if there was not room for them in the cottage, they stayed either in Alton, or at Chawton House, known to all of them as the Great House. It had been let for five years shortly before the Austens came to the village, but in 1813 it was free of tenants, and Edward brought his entire family to live there for five months while Godmersham was being repainted. It was a large, rambling Elizabethan house, much altered but, until very recently, little improved. Pevsner calls the sixteenth-century stables its best feature, saying of the house that it had been so much restored 'that it is no longer a pleasure to look at', and to a more recent visitor, Park Honan, who saw it before the hotel-makers stepped in, it was 'large, stuccoed, tapestried and chilly'. Jane, however, liked it, being inured to cold, and it is said that she would sit in the panelled embrasure above the porch, watching the visitors come and go. The church, which she would have seen from there and which she attended regularly, was almost totally rebuilt in 1871. The graves of Mrs Austen and Cassandra are in the churchyard.

One other member of the family became close to her, her niece Anna Lefroy, James's daughter by his first marriage, who lived in the delectable Wyards Farm. She was a lovely, wayward creature, and I agree with Anne-Marie Edwards's assessment that there was much of her in Emma Woodhouse, clever and attractive, but possessing 'the power of having rather too much her own way, and a disposition to think a little too well of herself'. She was an aspiring novelist, and would send her manuscripts to Jane for criticism, which was liberally forthcoming, but kind. Jane advised her to write only about people and places she knew: if one of her characters has to go to Ireland, don't go with him, because you don't know what it is like. Avoid clichés, and cut out incidents that do nothing to help the narrative forward. Make people behave consistently with their characters. Watch the class-

Anna Lefroy, the daughter of James Austen, who came to live near Chawton after her marriage and wrote novels which she submitted to her aunt for criticism. It is from their correspondence that we know most about Jane's method of literary composition.

Opposite Chawton House, Hampshire, the property of Jane's brother Edward. It lay only five minutes walk from her own house in Chawton village, and she would often watch the arrival of his guests and tenants from the window above the porch.

structure carefully. Get facts right – chronology, topography, genealogy. But the only published product of this admirable advice was a couple of children's books, and a continuation of *Sanditon*, of which Anna owned the manuscript.

As Jane was helping Anna, she was discovering in herself the energy and enthusiasm to resume her own writing. She had kept the three novels she wrote in her early twenties, *Sense and Sensibility*, *Pride and Prejudice* and *Northanger Abbey*, and she now revised them, but to what extent we shall never know, as the manuscripts of 'Elinor and Marianne', 'First Impressions' and 'Susan', as the three were originally called, have not survived. Almost the only hint is contained in a letter to Cassandra of 29 January 1813 about her revision of *Pride and Prejudice*: 'I have lop't and crop't so successfully that I imagine it must be rather shorter than S & S.' From this sentence and some internal evidence scholars have deduced that the revision was 'extensive' (Chapman), 'substantial' (Honan), 'radical' (Litz), but it is difficult to see how the novel could display so youthful a touch unless it had been there from the beginning. Its delicacy would not have survived major rewriting, even by its author, and the unity of the whole would have been lost had substantial variations from the original been introduced, suggested by Jane's later experiences of people and places. If her revision had been extensive, she would surely have noticed in her maturity that Darcy, given the fundamental excellence of his character, could never have behaved so discourteously to his host's guests or tried to ruin Jane Bennet's romance with his closest friend, Bingley, on the grounds that the Bennets had inferior connections. 'Lop't and crop't' suggests shortening, cutting out dead wood, not new growth. In her 'Advertisement' for a 1816 edition of *Northanger Abbey* (it was not in fact published until after her death), she asked the reader to 'bear in mind that thirteen years have passed since it was finished, many more since it was begun', which would put the final revision back to 1803, long before she came to Chawton. But the advertisement also suggests that there had been intermediate revision as well.

It is in any case a solid fact that all six of her novels issued from Chawton, three of them totally written there on that tiny table in that small room, while household chores were done around her and coaches thundered past outside. Seldom, even at Haworth, the Brontë's home, have great works of art been produced under such trying conditions. The chronology is worth repetition:

Mansfield Park: begun February 1811, finished June 1813
Emma: begun January 1814, finished March 1815
Persuasion: begun August 1815, finished August 1816

161

The publishing history is more erratic. The first of her books to find a publisher, Thomas Egerton, was *Sense and Sensibility* in 1811, but Jane had to pay for its publication and recover her expense by sales, less ten per-cent to the publisher. Egerton also published *Pride and Prejudice*, in 1812, this time at his own risk. *Mansfield Park* came out under the same imprint in 1814, and a second edition of seven hundred and fifty copies by Murray in 1816, of which four hundred and ninety-eight were remaindered in 1820. *Emma*, again with Murray, appeared in December 1815: five hundred and thirty-nine copies out of two thousand printed remained unsold in 1820. *Northanger Abbey* and *Persuasion* were published posthumously.

These details indicate how slow was the growth of her reputation, if it can be said that she had any reputation at all, because all her books were published anonymously in her lifetime, and only her family, a few close friends and the publishers knew her identity, or so she intended. In fact her name soon became one to drop. The Prince Regent's doctor had little difficulty in finding her out. Lady Robert Kerr was 'delighted with *Pride and Prejudice* before she knew who wrote it, for of course she knows now', Henry told her. To the Countess of Morely Jane wrote in

Opposite Fanny Knight, Edward's daughter and Jane's favourite niece; a drawing of Fanny painting a watercolour, probably by her aunt Cassandra. Jane wrote to her in 1817 shortly before her death, 'You are inimitable, irresistable. You are the delight of my life.' Later Fanny married Edward Knatchbull of Mersham-le-Hatch.

The Dining Parlour in Chawton Cottage where the Austen ladies met for meals and Jane Austen wrote on the little tripod table to the left of the photograph. Three of her published novels were rewritten there, and the other three composed, all within the space of seven years.

December 1815, 'Accept my thanks for the honour of your note, and for your kind disposition in favour of *Emma* ...' and signed herself, 'Your obliged and faithful servant J. Austen'. Locally, no very serious attempt was made to preserve her secret. Mrs Austen read *Pride and Prejudice* aloud to an audience which included the doleful Miss Benn, and Miss Prowting was given by Jane herself a very strong hint as to the authorship of *Emma*. But to the general public she was quite unknown, and never in all her life did she meet another writer. The first public acknowledgement of her work appeared in the obituary columns of the *Hampshire Chronicle and Courier* of 22 July 1817:

The house in College Street, Winchester, where Jane Austen died.

> On the 18th inst., at Winchester, Miss Jane Austen, youngest daughter of the late George Austen, Rector of Steventon, in Hampshire, and the Authoress of Emma, Mansfield Park, Pride and Prejudice and Sense and Sensibility. Her manners were most gentle; her affections ardent; her candor was not to be surpassed; and she lived and died as became a humble Christian.

The notice was probably drafted by one of her brothers, Henry or James.

Her health had been failing for some time, and while trying to write *Sanditon*, she had found it impossible for days on end, what with back pains and attacks of nausea. She probably had Addison's Disease, curable now, lethal then. She managed to leave her room for short periods, once riding the donkey instead of being pulled by it, and she could receive visitors, like Caroline and Anna, if they did not stay too long, but the local doctor advised that she should be put under more expert care. He strongly recommended Dr Lyford at Winchester, and arrangements were made to move her there. Winchester is only fifteen miles from Chawton, and with Cassandra and Martha Lloyd she made the journey by carriage on 24 May 1817, escorted on horseback by her brother Henry and Edward's son William Knight.

Rooms had been engaged for the three women at No. 8 College Street, adjoining the entrance to Winchester College and facing the wall that encircles the Cathedral close. It is a pretty little house with a bow window overlooking the headmaster's garden, but its rooms were small for an invalid who needed constant attention. She did manage to leave the house once, in a sedan chair, and promised her friends, but not herself, that she was getting better. In June she was worse, then rallied, and on 15 July, St Swithin's Day, she was merry enough to write a lampoon on Winchester's annual races. The first verse runs:

> When Winchester races first took their beginning
> It is said that good people forgot their old Saint
> Not applying at all for the leave of St Swithin
> And that William of Wykeham's approval was faint.

Three days later, on 18 July 1817, at about 4.30 in the morning, she died in Cassandra's arms.

How did she come to be buried in the Cathedral? It is barely possible that she personally asked the Dean when she knew herself to be dying. She was not a native of the City, nor a person of sufficient eminence to

Opposite The north aisle of Winchester Cathedral. The nearest figure stands by Jane's gravestone, seen *right* in detail.

In Memory of
JANE AUSTEN,
youngeſt daughter of the late
Revᵈ GEORGE AUSTEN,
formerly Rector of Steventon in this County
ſhe departed this Life on the 18ᵗʰ of July 1817,
aged 41, after a long illneſs ſupported with
the patience and the hopes of a Chriſtian.

The benevolence of her heart,
the ſweetneſs of her temper, and
the extraordinary endowments of her mind
obtained the regard of all who knew her, and
the warmeſt love of her intimate connections.

Their grief is in proportion to their affection
they know their loſs to be irreparable,
but in their deepeſt affliction they are confoled
by a firm though humble hope that her charity,
devotion, faith and purity, have rendered
her foul acceptable in the fight of her
REDEEMER.

deserve such an honour. Perhaps James or Henry persuaded the Chapter to allow it. 'But who *was* your sister?' 'She was called Jane Austen. She was forty-one years old. She was a writer of comic novels. She was a good woman and devout.' Whatever was said, the request was granted, and on 24 July she was buried in the north aisle. Henry observed that 'In the whole catalogue of its mighty dead, the Cathedral does not contain the ashes of a brighter genius or a sincerer Christian'. That would have been sufficient. But he composed for her grave-slab a more flowery epitaph that says much about her virtues but makes only one reference to her creative genius, in the line that reads, 'The extraordinary endowments of her mind'.

IX

ARCHITECTURE AND INTERIORS IN JANE AUSTEN'S NOVELS

Jane Austen's lifetime was a period of transformation in almost every branch of human activity – agriculture, art, literature, dress, architecture. There was large-scale emigration overseas, and from the country to the towns. The wars with France created a vast disturbance in the economy. It was the period of the cotton mill, the canal, of Robert Adam, Nash and Soane, of Arkwright and Coke of Norfolk, of Wellington and Nelson.

That England remained in other ways remarkably unchanged requires no better evidence than Jane Austen's novels. It is true that she ignored the spreading Midland cities, the urban and rural slums, and that politics and business, except subliminally, were of no interest to her. It is significant, for example, that she never invents a scene where two men are left alone together: she did not know how they talked, and what they talked about. Hers was a world of genteel, animated discourse between the sexes, strongly rooted in common sense and mutual affection. Their society was hardly affected by the American or French revolutions, and scarcely by the war. It was an England that was still primarily agricultural, before machinery had invaded the countryside or its soil had been wracked by chemicals or violated by the railways. If Jane Austen was conscious that the towns were rapidly expanding, she would be thinking only of the elegant new terraces of Bath, Cheltenham and London, not of Birmingham ('Birmingham', says Mrs Elton in *Emma*, 'is not a place to promise much. One has no great hopes for Birmingham. I always say there is something direful in the sound.')

The accumulation of wealth in the hands of an old aristocracy – ancient houses, well-tended land, heirlooms of every kind – provided the rising middle class with models of excellence when they were building and furnishing their own homes. Never had a building boom coincided with greater inventiveness. Never had sensitiveness to beauty been so widely spread. The small house borrowed ideas from the big house. Objects of everyday use like crockery, clothes, tools, chairs, were beautifully made, and in making them the craftsmen shared in the pleasure of the better-off who bought them. What is almost inexplicable is their unerring sense of colour and proportion. Nothing in the middle-class house was strident, nothing ungainly, nothing shoddy. Never had the building and furniture trades been so efficient. Everything was made to last; everything functioned as intended. A man without natural discrimination need not worry how he furnished his house, for there was nothing on sale which could disfigure it.

Mechanical inventions, until the steam-engine came, did not affect the placidity of southern towns any more than the war affected the average home. Architectural development refined what was still basi-cally a classical taste. There was no abrupt change in building style comparable to what happened after 1820, but in the last quarter of the eighteenth century there was a feeling that Palladianism had said everything it had to say, and the cultured world was receptive for something new. They embraced Robert Adam for some twenty years, welcoming his delicate, pastel decoration with motifs drawn from the Pompeiian and Etruscan, his curving of room-ends into apses, his use of light ironwork in balustrades, fire-grates and door handles, and of graceful columns within the house. It was a triumph of simplicity and lightness of touch. Then came the new Gothic, the Regency, the rustic and the exotic. By 1817, when Jane Austen died, there was a great variety of building styles, and though it was often on a large scale, like Nash's Regent's Park or the newer crescents of Clifton and Cheltenham, the design was always governed by a purity of line and form, sometimes whimsical and playful, like Brighton Pavilion or the villas which Nash was erecting for a new class of client in suburbs or along the sea front, some of them little bigger than cottages, architectural toys, but they always played tribute to a classical origin, a habit difficult to shake off. Balconies were extruded from the façades with tentlike canopies above them and French windows carried to the floor, all in the spirit of cheerfulness, elegance and refinement, like women's dresses when the formal gown gave way to the simple 'Greek' style of clinging, high-waisted, shift-like muslin dresses that Jane Austen wore in her youth.

How much of this architectural change did she notice? Not, one surmises, a great deal when it was happening to public buildings. They were simply buildings for use, like a town hall or church. As for domestic buildings, there is evidence in *Sanditon* that she had noticed the spread of the Regency fashion, perhaps in Cheltenham where she spent three weeks with Cassandra in May 1816, but there is nothing in her writings to suggest that she had even heard of Robert Adam. She may never have seen an Adam interior except at Mersham-le-Hatch, which was

Previous page Royal York Crescent, Clifton, in Bristol. the crescent (said to be the longest in Europe) was begun in 1791 but was not completed till after the Napoleonic wars. Building continued throughout the Austens' short residence in the town.

Opposite The Kennet and Avon Canal where it passes the site of the old Rectory in Kintbury, Berkshire. Jane spent happy months there with her friends the Fowles. This stretch of the canal (which eventually reached Bath) was completed in 1797, and she saw it under construction.

The staircase at Stoneleigh Abbey, certainly the grandest house the Austens stayed in, for a week in 1806. The stucco reliefs are of superb quality, the work of an Italian craftsman.

a poor one. Of the new Gothic she saw a good example at Adlestrop Park, which Sanderson Miller had converted for her Leigh cousins in the 1760s. From there she would almost certainly have visited Daylesford, a beautiful house built for Warren Hastings by Samuel Pepys Cockerell that displays in its interior oriental motifs (for Cockerell was an East India Company man) which would have given Jane a notion of the new taste for the exotic.

Her own taste remained conventional. 'She was born in the eighteenth century', wrote David Cecil, 'and, spiritually speaking, she stayed there.' She shared with Fanny Price a love of orderliness, the 'elegance, propriety, regularity and harmony' of Mansfield Park, contrasted with the disorder and turmoil of Fanny's parents' house in Portsmouth.

She was neat in her habits, like her handwriting. Once she wrote to Cassandra with displeasure at the slovenliness of her sister-in-law Mary, James's wife: 'She is not tidy enough in her appearance; she has no dressing-gown to sit up in; her curtains are all too thin, and things are not in that comfort and style about her which are necessary to make such a situation an enviable one' (Mary had just had a baby). On the other hand, Jane had no great love of grandeur. As a guest she had been inside some of the loveliest houses in England – Stoneleigh, Godmersham, The Vyne, Hackwood – and as a tourist she had entered several others like Warwick Castle and perhaps Blenheim. But her interest in them was soon exhausted, like Elizabeth Bennet's, who owned that 'she was tired of great houses; after going over so many, she really had no pleasure in fine carpets or satin curtains'. The late Duke of Wellington, himself an architect and the first President of the Jane Austen Society, wrote that she 'cared nothing for the visual arts', but that cannot be entirely true. She looked about her. Like Charlotte Heywood (in *Sanditon*) visiting Lady Denham's great house, she would notice that the sitting-room was well-proportioned and well-furnished, 'though it was furniture rather originally good and extremely well kept, than new and showy'. In her descriptions of other fictional interiors, like Sotherton's, she is careful to note decoration and furniture more than painting and ornaments, and date them approximately, from which it is clear that she never entered a room without it making some definite impression on her. If in her novels she did not linger over the detail, it was to avoid elaboration at the expense of the story. She advised Anna Lefroy, the burgeoning novelist: 'Your descriptions are often more minute than will be liked. You give too many particulars of right hand and left.'

But she could hardly mention a building without endowing it by deft touches with a distinctive personality. She described small houses even more carefully than she did people. Like Hunsford Parsonage (*Pride and Prejudice*), 'rather small, but well-built and convenient, and everything was fitted up and arranged with neatness and consistency'; or Randalls (*Emma*), 'two living rooms each side of a middle passage with facing doors'; or Woodston Parsonage (*Northanger Abbey*), 'a prettily shaped room, the windows reaching to the ground, and the view from them pleasant'. Barton Cottage (*Sense and Sensibility*) is pieced together with some irony:

Though small it was comfortable, but as a cottage it was defective, for the building was regular, the roof was tiled, the window shutters were not painted green, nor were the walls covered with honeysuckle. A narrow passage led directly through the house into the garden behind. On each side of the entrance was a sitting-room, about sixteen feet square, and beyond them were the offices and the stairs. Four bedrooms and two garrets formed the rest of the house. It had not been built many years and was in good repair.

Later we learn that there was room for the Dashwoods to have one guest to stay, that the stairs were dark and narrow, that a defective chimney filled the kitchen with smoke, and that the ceilings were low and crooked. No mention is made here, nor in the description of any other house, of lavatories or how people bathed. Nor is any distinction made in the style of smaller English houses from one English region to another. From Kent to Devon they could be interchangeable.

The set-piece houses were not for her. Here is Mr Collins escorting Elizabeth Bennet and the Lucases for their first meeting with Lady Catherine de Bourgh at Rosings:

> As the weather was fine, they had a pleasant walk of about half a mile across the park. Every park has its beauty and its prospects, and Elizabeth saw much to be pleased with, though she could not be in such raptures as Mr Collins expected the scene to inspire, and was but slightly affected by his enumeration of the windows in front of the house, and his relation of what the glazing altogether had originally cost Sir Lewis de Bourgh.
>
> When they ascended the steps to the hall, Maria [Lucas's] alarm was every moment increasing, and even Sir William [Lucas] did not look perfectly calm. Elizabeth's courage did not fail her ... From the entrance hall, of which Mr Collins pointed out, with a rapturous air, the fine proportions and finished ornaments, they followed the servants through an ante-chamber, to the room where Lady Catherine, her daughter and Mrs Jenkinson were sitting. Her ladyship, with great condescension, arose to receive them.

There are few better illustrations of the art with which Jane Austen uses a house and its surroundings to manipulate her people and reveal their characters. In turn we see Rosings through the eyes of Mr Collins, Elizabeth Bennet, Miss Lucas and Lady Catherine, and slowly the house itself takes shape – its site, the dazzling display of its windows, its steps to the front door, and the series of rooms which gradually admit the visitor to the mistress's formidable presence. It is assumed that the reader will share Elizabeth's opinion of all this flummery and, like her, refuse to be impressed.

Not so with Mr Darcy's Pemberley. It is a 'large handsome stone building standing well on rising ground', set in a beautiful park ten miles round, and its interior is wonderfully elegant, furnished with antique and modern pieces and paintings. Elizabeth is moved by it, and although Rosings and Pemberley are of much the same degree of architectural distinction (Rosings perhaps Palladian, Pemberley Jacobean), we are persuaded to dislike the first and admire the second, because in Jane's eyes the character of a house is strongly influenced by the character of its occupants. Mansfield Park is probably Palladian too, but its outward appearance is sketched but lightly. It is loveable because Fanny Price loves it, while Sotherton is unloveable because it belongs to the absurd Mr Rushworth who will marry the unpleasant Maria Bertram. It is Elizabethan, 'a large, regular brick building – heavy but respectable looking, and has many good rooms. It is ill-placed . . . The rooms are all lofty, and many large, and amply furnished in the taste of fifty years back [which would make it William Kent], with shining floors, solid mahogany, rich damask, marble, gilding and carving, each handsome in its own way.' Even Fanny is disappointed by the James II chapel. Admiration for Sotherton comes grudgingly.

Chawton House, and its neighbouring church where Mrs Austen and Cassandra are buried. The Elizabethan house, five minutes walk from Chawton Cottage, was inherited by Edward Austen from the Knights of Godmersham.

Donwell Abbey, I believe, was Jane's ideal home, as it was for Emma, its future mistress, 'as she viewed the respectable size and style of the building, its suitable, becoming, characteristic situation, low and sheltered ... covering a good deal of ground, rambling and irregular', and it is almost the only house that Jane could imagine herself living in, if the Austen fortune had stretched that high, because it was intimately wedded to the countryside, a manor house in the oldest sense. No town house, in Bath or London, is mentioned with any affection at all, unless one counts Mrs Jennings's house off Portman Square, 'handsome and handsomely fitted up', words which, for Jane Austen, had become a cliché. Smaller middle-class houses in villages attract muted praise, like the Woodhouses' Hartfield, 'modern and well-built', but in *The Watsons* Mr Tomlinson, a banker who has built a house on the outskirts of a small town, is ridiculed because he calls it 'a country seat'. Once again, architecture is used to suggest character and point a moral.

Nikolaus Pevsner claimed that Jane Austen 'is without exception vague, when it came to describing buildings', as if she had deprived him of something that the reader needed to know. But she did not want us to catch the next train to Highbury. She was taking for granted the social background that was so familiar to her first readers but must be imagined or accepted by us. They knew that the presence of servants in a room could be ignored ('there was no interruption and no witnesses [of Fanny's greeting to her brother at Mansfield Park], unless the servants ... could be called such'), what other function a 'breakfast room' had, and how meals were kept hot when they had to be carried from a distant kitchen. Her readers could also be expected to know (and so can we, since many such houses have been opened to public view) what a Palladian portico, or a long gallery, or a parlour, or a spiral staircase, looked like, and there was no need to particularise the contents of a room when her main concern was with the relationship between the people in it. Besides, she did not feel competent to describe works of art or the minutiae of architectural or decorative styles. If she had been, such a parade of learning would not have enhanced her story, but dulled it.

There was another reason. She did not want her houses to be recognised. A great deal of harmless pleasure has been generated by finding the 'originals' for this Austen house or that, and it is always the larger houses that attract attention. Pemberley 'must be' Chatsworth because the landscaping of the park fits it well, ignoring the improbability that Jane ever saw it, or if she did, it was long after 'First Impressions' had already delineated Pemberley beyond alteration. Rosings 'is clearly based' on Chevening near Westerham in Kent, because Rosings is also near Westerham, and Jane's second cousin became Rector of Chevening the year after *Pride and Prejudice* was published. The trouble is that Mr Collins's parsonage lay half-a-mile from the great house, while the Rev. Austen's, like the present vicarage, lay close beside it. Nor is there any proof that Jane Austen did more than pass the house on her way to Godmersham. Barton Park in *Sense and Sensibility* is identified with Pynes, north of Exeter, by its owner Lord Iddesleigh ('I am writing in the room in which Sir John Middleton ate his dinner'), and it might well be so, were it not that the novel was drafted 'in its present form' in 1797, and Jane Austen went nowhere near Exeter till the family's holiday to Dawlish in 1802. David Grey, in his excellent contribution on Topography to *The Jane Austen Handbook* which he edited, explores and gently explodes many other such attributions. Easton Neston, one of the most beautiful houses in England, is claimed as the original Mansfield Park, but it lies on the wrong side of Northampton. So it 'must be' Cottesbrooke. And so on.

Opposite above Chevening, Kent, which Jane may have known on her visits to Sevenoaks. It has been identified with Rosings in *Pride and Prejudice*, with which it has some resemblance.

Opposite below Pynes, north of Exeter, Devon, which has been identified with Barton Park in *Sense and Sensibility*.

Jane Austen was scrupulous about her topography. Distances between named towns are accurate to a mile, and when she chooses as a location real places, like the streets of Bath, she is unfaultable. But 'a large handsome stone (or brick) building standing well on rising ground' could be found in many parts of England, and certainly in the imagination of any novelist. If there is a real village which can bear comparison with an imaginary Austen village, it is Great Bookham in Surrey as a model for Highbury in *Emma*: and if there is one great house which coloured her description of several others, it is Godmersham, near Canterbury in Kent, where she spent many of the happiest days of her life with her brother.

Picture Acknowledgements

We are grateful to the following individuals or institutions for permission to make use of the illustrations listed (by page-number) against their names:

Map: Rita Wütrich
Alwyn Austen 27 (right)
Avon County Libraries: Bath Central Library 86, 97, 99, 100
Mrs Oliver Bellasis 36
Michael Boyle 40
British Museum 80, 124
Fashion Research Centre, Bath 17, 31
Rev. Martin Gillham, Kintbury 149

Hampshire County Council Archives 29, 44–5
Captain and Mrs David Husband 178 (top)
Jane Austen Memorial Trust, Chawton: 19 (top and bottom), 20, 24 (top and bottom), 25, 35 (top), 62, 68 (top left), 132 (top), 161, 163, 175
Museum of London 15
National Library of Scotland 67
National Portrait Gallery, London 27 (left)
Tudor House Museum, Southampton 131
Victoria Art Gallery, Bath 84
Richard Whitelaw 154, 156
Yale Center for British Art, Paul Mellon Collection 58–9

Bibliography

Austen, Caroline. *Reminiscences of Caroline Austen.* Jane Austen Society, 1986

Austen, Jane. *Sense and Sensibility.*
Pride and Prejudice.
Mansfield Park.
Emma.
Persuasion.
Northanger Abbey.
Lady Susan, The Watsons, Sanditon. Penguin Classics, 1974
Juvenilia (with Juvenilia of Charlotte Brontë). Penguin Classics, 1986;
Letters. Two vols, ed. R. W. Chapman, 2nd ed. Oxford, 1952

Austen-Leigh, James Edward. *A Memoir of Jane Austen.* 1869

Austen-Leigh, Richard Arthur and William. *Jane Austen: Her Life and Letters.* 1913. Revised and enlarged edit. *Jane Austen: A Family Record* ed. Deirdre le Faye, British Library, 1989

Bussby, Frederick. *Jane Austen in Winchester.* Friends of Winchester Cathedral, 1984

Cecil, David. *A Portrait of Jane Austen.* Constable, 1978

Chapman, R. W. *Jane Austen: Facts and Problems.* The Clark Lectures, Oxford, 1948

Edwards, Anne-Marie. *In the Steps of Jane Austen.* 2nd edition. Arcady Books, 1985

Fowles, John. *A Short History of Lyme Regis* Dovecot Press, 1982

Freeman, Jean. *Jane Austen in Bath.* Jane Austen Society, 1983

Gadd, David. *Georgian Summer: The Rise and Development of Bath.* Countryside Books, 1987

Grey, J. David. Ed. *The Jane Austen Handbook.* Athlone Press, London, 1986

Hill, Constance. *Jane Austen: Her Homes and her Friends.* John Lane, 1902

Honan, Park. *Jane Austen: Her Life.* Weidenfeld & Nicolson, 1987

Hubback, J. H. & E. *Jane Austen's Sailor Brothers.* John Lane, 1906

Ison, Walter. *The Georgian Buildings of Bath.* Kingshead Press, Bath, 1980

Jane Austen Memorial Trust. *Jane Austen's Houses.* (Guidebook), 1988

Lane, Maggie. *Jane Austen's England.* Hale, 1986; *A Charming Place: Bath in the Life and Times of Jane Austen.* Millstream Books, Bath, 1988

Laski, Marghanita. *Jane Austen.* Thames & Hudson, 1975

Mowl, Tim and Earnshaw, Brian. *John Wood, Architect of Obsession.* Millstream Books, Bath, 1988

Ordnance Survey. *Historical Map to Georgian Bath*

Pevsner, Nikolaus. *Buildings of England.* North Somerset & Bristol, Penguin, 1986, Hampshire (with David Lloyd), Penguin, 1985

Turner, Roger. *Capability Brown.* Weidenfeld & Nicolson, 1985

Waldron-Smithers, David. *Jane Austen in Kent.* Hurtwood Publications, 1981

Watkins, Susan. *Jane Austen's Town and Country Style.* Thames & Hudson, 1990

Index

The page-numbers in italics refer to the illustrations.

ABBREVIATIONS: J.A., Jane Austen; P.&P., *Pride and Prejudice*; S.&S., *Sense and Sensibility*; N.A., *Northanger Abbey*; P., *Persuasion*; E., *Emma*; M.P., *Mansfield Park*.